RECRUITMENT AGENCY REVOLUTION

Revealed - The closely guarded secrets to how recruitment agencies make their vast fortunes; more importantly, how you can have your share of this £35 billion industry!

Joel Davis

DISCLAIMER AND COPYRIGHT

"One day, you will wake up, and there won't be *any more time to do the things you've always wanted."*

DO IT NOW!

—Paulo Coelho

TABLE OF CONTENTS

A Special Thanks:

My team, Jessica, Smitha, Moriam, James, and Jerome, has been working with me for over ten years, supporting the cause to open up recruitments' £35 billion industry to the many, not just a few.

A heartfelt thank you for sticking by me through the good times and the bad...

The Good Times:

- Out of 1,056 contestants, coming 3rd in the public vote for Richard Branson's Voom Pitch competition for the company that had the most innovative business programme so close and yet so far...Maybe next time.

- Launching our first TV commercial, which was made in-house. This was truly incredible because it looked like a high-budget TV commercial, but it was done on a shoestring budget.

- Receiving over 120 testimonials from our amazing clients and customers. So much so that I was able to dedicate an entire chapter of the book to these testimonials.

- Creating, building, and launching our own recruitment CRM software programme, which has been designed specifically for people new to recruitment.

- Helping Recruitment Startup Consultancy Ltd to remain the UK's No.1 recruitment start-up agency that is taking the recruitment industry by storm. Opening up the industry to people from all ages, backgrounds, and walks of life.

And The Bad:

- Helping search for my car keys in the thick snow in Surrey Street Market, in the dead of night!

- Breaking down in the fast lane of the motorway. Risking life and limb in a hired van on the way to a business exhibition, almost giving the RAC roadside mechanic a cardiac arrest!

- Working sometimes till midnight to build up to ten websites per week while still being on hand to support existing clients with any questions and queries on their website.

- Having a master craftsman on the team to remodel a very expensive boardroom table that was way too big for our meeting room.

- Everyone keeping a straight face, with my constant flow of *'champagne ideas'* that had *'ginger bear'* results!

Once again, thanks a million. One *year,* I will get it right!

ACKNOWLEDGMENT

I joined the recruitment industry back in the late 70s.

At the time, I worked for a company called Atlas employment agency in Buckingham Palace Gate, London; this was the company's flagship branch.

During those days, it wasn't unusual for clients to phone in with their vacancies, and of course, whoever picked up the phone first got the vacancy to work on and invariably earned the commission.

Then, I worked in an office with two experienced recruitment consultants, and the speed at which they picked up the phone was like working with wild Bill Hickok and Wyatt Earp. I couldn't get a look-in.

As in the old gunslinger movies in those days, you had the quick and the dead. If you weren't making placements and generating money, you were quickly shown the door.

So, within a couple of weeks in the business, I quickly realised that I was drinking in the last chance saloon of keeping my job; I had to come up with a way of getting to the phone fast.

The phone system they had back then was the PABX, and from where I was sitting, I noticed that just before the phone rang, the switchboard in the cupboard beside me would make a slight clicking sound.

Just before the phone would ring in the office, I would hear this faint click, and therefore it wasn't long before I started beating the other consultants to the draw every time.

Now that the tables had turned, these two consultants complained bitterly to the branch manager, saying that somehow or another I was using some kind of *sixth sense*, as, how else would I know that the phone was going to ring before it actually did.

But as I was bringing in more money than the other two consultants had ever brought in, plus the manager bonus was based on my sales, she reluctantly left me alone.

However, there was a problem that these consultants knew would eventually trip me up, even get me sacked.

You see, my typing was painfully slow, and for every placement I made, I would have to type up an offer letter, send out terms and conditions, along with an invoice.

At the time, unbeknown to me, at the end of the month, the branch would be audited by the Managing Director, and if anyone's paperwork weren't up to scratch, they would be shown the door.

A week before the audit, the branch manager informed me of this audit.

The consultants just smirked and said to me, '*it was nice knowing you, kiddo!*'

Ouch!

I was at a complete loss as to what to do.

To make matters worse, this company had a policy that no one could stay working in the office after 6:30 pm.

They were paranoid that someone would try to photocopy their clients' database and candidates with the view to poaching their business.

At the time, my wife would meet me at work, and we would go home together; we were both twenty, just married and seeing her was the highlight of my day... Ahh, young love

Back to my story, one evening, my wife turned up and noticed that I was looking a little stressed out.

Is everything OK? she lovingly asked.

I said, not really. I have this stack of offer letters to type up, invoices to go out, plus several CVs that need editing, and it has to be done within the week.

She replied, *'can I do anything to help.'*

So, I said sure. I had to confirm a couple of interviews before we left the office, and so I showed her what needed to be done, sat her down in front of the office typewriter (no computers back then) and left her to get on with it.

After ten minutes, my wife came over and said, *'do you have anything else that needs doing?'*

I said, no, but you have to do the full pile of offer letters and invoices.

She said, '*well, I have edited all the CVs, typed up the offer letters and completed the invoices ready for posting.*'

I was completely stunned. Now I knew my wife was a fast typist, extremely bright and well organised. The speed at which she had got everything done and dusted left me speechless.

Knowing that my wife would be able to support me with the admin side of the business before I left the office allowed me to concentrate all my efforts on making placements, which resulted in me making even more commission.

On the day of the audit, the consultants and manager had brought in a bottle of wine to celebrate my departure, as they were dead sure that I hadn't completed the paperwork, and therefore I was going to be given my marching orders.

After completing the audit, the Managing Director called me into her office and said that not only had I generated the most revenue throughout the whole company but went on to say that she had never seen anyone's paperwork so up-to-date and so neatly typed up.

"Well, Mr Davis, I am promoting you to the branch manager, and your first duty will be to tell the existing manager that today was going to be her last day."

She then just waltzed out of the office and left me to get on with it.

To say my conversation with the manager and the staff was a little awkward would be an understatement.

Nevertheless, it needed to be done, and after the manager had left, the other two consultants were as good as gold.

Now I have included this account, in the acknowledgement section of this book, as a way of showing my appreciation for how my wife helped me at the start of my career in recruitment.

Thanks, Av xxx

CONNECT WITH JOE

FOREWORD

When Joel asked me to write the foreword to his book, I was humbled and truly honoured.

I know Joel has connections within the recruitment industry that he could have approached; he could even have asked one of his seven figures a year recruitment agencies that he had set up to write the foreword to this book.

But he asked me as he felt my experience of how I started my home-based recruitment agency will resonate more with his target audience.

So here goes.

I actually met Joel a year before I started my recruitment agency. I had attended one of his workshop events to initially find out more about what was involved in having a home-based recruitment agency.

And I was truly blown away.

The idea that his company's goal was to help ordinary people from all backgrounds and walks of life have to a slice of recruitments £35 billion industry struck a chord with me.

When he said how much the investment would be to get started, my heart sunk, as I didn't have the money to invest.

What made the experience even more painful was that he would invite people who wanted to start for a one-to-one meeting to sign up at the end of his workshop presentation.

And when I saw people excitedly coming back into the boardroom, all with their large bright white laminated tote bag, with Recruitment Startups training products inside, my heart sunk even further.

This experience stayed with me until a year or so later.

Fortunately, I came into some money and immediately contacted Joel to make my investment and get started, and within six weeks of being in business, yes, just six weeks, I was able to leave my full-time job.

One of the first thing that I learned from his one-to-one training was how to shift my mindset to see that I was more than capable of being the boss of my own recruitment agency.

You see, I had been working for a leading hospitality organisation, and at times it felt like I was invisible.

To make matters worse, I was expected to train new Chefs who came into the company, and before I knew it, they became my boss.

However, when I joined the recruitment startups coaching programme, although I started as a home-based recruitment agency, I quickly moved from a home-based to having an office and employing a team of recruitment consultants to work in the business.

At times I had to pinch myself to make sure that I wasn't dreaming.

Moving on to this book, "Recruitment Agency Revolution." I can't believe how much detailed information from his coaching programme Joel has included in this book.

There are three chapters in the book that lays out in great detail the whole recruitment process, from finding jobs to sourcing suitable candidates for these positions, placing them with a client and getting paid.

I know for a fact that you can't find this information on starting a recruitment agency outside the pages of this book.

If you are in any doubt about whether or not this is the right business opportunity for you, look at the hundred plus client and customer testimonials in the book.

Coming back to Joel's coaching and training programme. His one-to-one training helped me realise that I could live life on my terms and be the captain of my own ship.

As opposed to just being a galley rower, not having a clue in which direction the ship was headed (actually, I was more of a galley chef than a rower, but still no idea of where the ship was headed).

Has the journey been easy? No, it has not.

At times, having people working for you is not without its challenges; however, Joel was always on hand to help manage any issues that came up.

Am I working as hard as when I was working as a chef? I would say more differently than harder, using my brains, not just my hands.

Was it worth the investment? Yes, most definitely, especially as I can keep 100% of the profit that I make. I only wished I was in the position to start my recruitment agency earlier.

If you are still undecided once you have read this book, I would strongly encourage you to attend one of his free webinar events to further details of what is contained in their masterclass coaching and training programme.

You also learn why, like me, you don't need any previous business or recruitment experience to get started.

Then to book a call with him. You may have to wait a few weeks to get on the phone with Joel directly. If that is the case, I will encourage you to get on the phone with one of his team, that I have all personally met.

They have worked with him for over a decade, and they are more than capable of answering any questions you may have about getting started.

Finally, Joel and his team have helped turn my life around, not only financially, but by giving me the confidence and belief in my ability to be the boss of my very own recruitment agency and never again having to feel like a second-class citizen as I was made to feel at my previous job.

Once again, a special thank you to Joel and all the team at Recruitment Startup Consultancy.

Brenda Falconer

Managing Director

P.S. "I still can't believe Joel asked me to write this foreword. I have even ordered a few copies for my close friends and family...so that they can know more about this opportunity, and if I'm honest to show them the foreword I had the privilege of writing for this book."

INTRODUCTION

What is Life If Not a Gamble

One Friday evening, I was driving home from work, and scrolling through the channels on my car radio for a song I could sing along to, as you do; or is it just me?

Anyway, one of the stations was playing an old Kenny Rogers song, "The Gambler."

The song brought back fond memories of when I was on holiday in Jamaica with my family, attending a karaoke event.

Someone had chosen this song 'the gambler,' much to the dismay of most of the locals, including tourists who mainly were only interested in singing along to one of Bob Marley's hit songs.

For those not familiar with Kenny Rogers, he is a country and western singer, some of his top hits were 'Lady, Lucille, and She believes in me.'

The late Kenny Roger's rendition of the Gambler is reportedly not only one of the greatest country and western songs ever recorded; it is also a contender for the best worldwide hit of all time.

It was released over four decades ago. Coincidently, about the same time that I was starting my career in the recruitment industry.

But I digress...

As I was listening to this tourist effectively butchering this song, I couldn't help but notice how the lyrics displayed on the screen had some powerful object lessons for people I meet who are looking to start their own recruitment agency.

This song's lyrics especially resonated with those who tended to hold back from getting started because of being too afraid to take a risk (or, in the song's words, to take a gamble).

The song starts with the words:

"If you're gonna play the game, boy, You gotta learn to play it right."

The point here is the importance of understanding your market, industry, and products to have a fair chance of success.

And to do this effectively, you need to have a business coach in your corner, working alongside you to guide you every step of the way.

A business coach is a professional who knows the ins and outs of running a business.

This includes (but is not limited to) advice about finding additional funding, increasing your company's sales and most importantly, being available to give you one-to-one hands-on training and support with areas of the business you are unsure about.

Some years ago, a friend of mine who worked as a painter and decorator won a tender to re-wallpaper the main hall of a stately home.

The reason why he had to tender for this job was that the walls were to be covered with an extremely expensive velvet fabric wallpaper with a mural portrait that a contemporary artist had created.

As he arrived at the job, he was led to the room where the wallpaper was to be hung and noticed that one roll of wallpaper had been pasted up, but it was ripped.

So, the owners asked him to strip it off and replace it with a brand-new mural, which would have meant that they had wasted thousands of pounds on the first one that had to be thrown away.

Tactfully, he asked: ‘so what went wrong?’ The wife said that her husband, much to her protestation, decided to do the job himself.

She had argued that they should get a professional, especially as the wallpaper was so expensive.

Also, as the mural was made to measure, there was no margin for error, but she concluded that her argument fell on deaf ears.

He quickly butted in, ‘yes, but it’s still your fault.’

He said that he had watched a YouTube video on how to hang this type of wallpaper, and the job looked fairly straightforward.

He continued, as the wall was not square, and the section to be covered was over four metres high; he had fastened a plumb line, sometimes known as a plumb bob, to the wall.

This is a tool used by builders and painters to find the true vertical of a wall.

So, as instructed by the YouTube video, he pasted the wall with glue, climbed the ladder, fixed the top section of the wallpaper, let the rest of it slowly unfold, then painstakingly married the wallpaper up to the hanging plumb line. Then proceeded to descend the ladder smoothing the paper out to the edges with his paper-hangers brush.

As he was halfway down the ladder, to his shock, he saw his wife with the plumb line in her hand, tugged slightly to one side.

She said that the line was hanging loosely and didn't look straight but assured him it was now dead straight.

Needless to say, it wasn't, and the wallpaper ripped when he attempted to straighten it out.

Hence, they had now hired him as the professional to do the job properly.

When doing any DIY project around the home, more often than not, your best bet is to leave it up to the experts. 'If you buy cheap, you pay twice.'

Building a successful business is no different. You need to have someone who is an expert in the field to either set things up for you or even do it with you to make sure it is done correctly. To get it wrong like this couple can be costly.

One of the most important aspects of planning your road map to success is to have a business plan coupled with a set of short and long-term goals.

Setting goals is the first step in turning the invisible into the visible.

Having a goal always implies an action that has to be taken to reach it; so, your goal-setting process leads to effectively using the products in our masterclass coaching and training programme to learn '*how to play the game and how to play to win.*'

Our Recruitment Agency Revolution business programme comes with a coach to guide your every step of the way.

My team of recruitment experts, who have worked with me for over ten years, will also be on hand along with me to answer any queries you may have with following our unique recruitment agency business model.

The song continues: ***"You got to know when to hold `em, know when to fold `em," (cards that is)***

Starting a business, to a degree, is a gamble, and if you aren't prepared to take risks, then starting a business may not be right for you. Therefore, it's the best folding by throwing in your cards.

There is no question that owning your own business is a risky proposition.

However, with risk comes reward. Put another way, the better you are at managing risk, the more rewards you can look to reap.

Being your own boss is fundamentally linked to risk-taking. You'll need to invest some of your personal capital and time into getting started.

However, these would be calculated risks, which involve a series of knowns that allows you to reasonably predict the odds of success.

In other words, you have the ability to stack the deck in your favour.

For example, as previously mentioned, having the support from someone with over 40 years' experience in recruitment, who has helped numerous people to start their own recruitment agency and is willing to provide you with hands-on training to get started, I would say, is a calculable risk worth taking.

In business, it's considered risky to have the majority of one's work and income come from a single customer – all your eggs in one basket, so to speak.

Yet, as an employee, working for 'the man' effectively, that's what you are signed up to.

When starting a recruitment agency, it doesn't take long before you have several clients paying to use your service, making having your own business far less of a risky option.

I would much prefer to have the revenue provided for my family and me coming from several different clients using my service, with me having the ability to scale up instead of putting my faith in a single source of income from a job.

The next verse of the song is ***"Know when to walk away."***

If you are the type of person who spends ten minutes in line trying to decide whether to have an Almond Milk

Honey Flat White or an Iced White Chocolate Mocha, you better start to sharpen your decision-making skills.

The truth is this, so many people think about starting a business; they even register a domain name and build a website but never do anything about actually getting started.

If you have a business and it's not making any money, it's a hobby and not a business.

People often tell themselves, 'I will start my business as soon as I' (fill in the blank)

...have enough savings in the bank; ...when the kids are off to college; ...as soon as my partner secures that promotion; ...in two-years-time when I finish my degree.

There are endless things you can "wait for." However, if you delay, you will find one-year morphs into five.

Then one day, you will wake up, and there won't be any more time to do the things you've always wanted.

There's no perfect time to start a business, just like there's no ideal time to start a family.

However, the longer you wait, the fewer quality years you have to build a successful enterprise.

So, no more excuses, you should do it now.

"And know when to run."

There are two inherent biases in the human mind that skew our perceptions of risk.

The first is that people tend to exaggerate the possibility of failure. In raw estimates (with limited numerical data), they are pessimistically predicting failure more than real situations would warrant.

The second is that people also greatly exaggerate the consequences of those failures; we envision the worst-case scenario when the reality is far more manageable.

Keep this in mind if you fall into the trap of imagining the negative possibilities associated with your risks.

And it has a lot to do with developing a positive mental attitude, as the saying goes:

"The pessimist complains about the wind; the optimist expects it to change; the realist adjusts the sails."

The next verse offers some sage advice. ***"You never count your money when you`re sittin` at the table. There`ll be time enough for countin` when the dealin`s done."***

The truth is that sometimes, you take more risk working as an employee in a job than having your own business.

I recall working as a director for one recruitment agency, where the owner decided to sell the company without giving any of the directors the heads up.

Even though I was responsible for bringing in most of the contracts into the business, and therefore at the time, I felt secure in my job (*sitting comfortably at the table so to speak*).

To make the company's bottom line look healthier for the sale, I was let go.

The Chairman of this recruitment agency told the new owners that I was just an account manager.

It wasn't until the new owners started seeing the business dropping off, did they realise how pivotal I was to the company, but I had moved on by that time.

This experience taught me a sobering lesson. When working as an employee in any company, you are more often than not at the mercy of one person (your boss), who has the power to decide your fate.

As was the case with this company and me, and even though I cared for the owner's

company, the truth was that he cared less about me.

Well, lesson learned. *'Good times become good memories, and bad times become good lessons in life.'*

The song continues ***'that every gambler knows the secret for surviving.'***

Many have wondered what is the secret to survival or having a successful business?

Well, first and foremost, as previously mentioned, you need to have a mentor or a coach, someone to take you by the hand and show you step-by-step how to succeed.

To quote the business guru Tony Robbins:

"If you want to be successful, find someone who has achieved the results you want and copy what they do, and you'll achieve the same results."

In this book, I will be revealing to you the closely guarded secrets of how recruitment agencies make their vast fortunes, and more importantly, how you can have your share of this £35 billion industry.

And that's without you having any previous recruitment or business experience whatsoever.

When setting up a home-based recruitment agency, it's important you know that you cannot gain all the necessary skills by yourself; this information is not available on the open market.

As with our stately homeowners, you won't find the answers going down the YouTube rabbit hole!

Even if you have experience working as a recruitment consultant, sourcing all the legal documents required to get started, terms of business, employment contracts, CRM software, policies, and procedures will be a very time-consuming and costly exercise.

Working with my company is like having a highly experienced partner in your corner.

Clients on our programme are provided with a tried and tested business model, effectively a road map helping them to get to where they want to in the shortest time possible.

Our new start-ups also receive weekly coaching calls and advice specifically designed to help them confidently navigate the rough terrain of running a business.

As they say in the coaching world, one plus one equals done.

The business start-up masterclass coaching and consultancy programme is a 90-day step-by-step business model showing you how to set up your home-based recruitment agency literally from scratch.

The framework for this programme is new, unique, and easy to follow. It is a business model designed to disrupt the recruitment industry completely, allowing anyone who joins to quickly and easily have a share of this multi-billion-pound industry.

The next verse Is ***"knowin' what to throw away And knowin' what to keep."***

This verse highlights the importance of setting priorities in your business.

Recently I had one of my new start-up say she was struggling to find time to work on her recruitment agency.

I said that most of our new start-ups work on their recruitment agency a couple of evenings a week to start with and as and when they are earning the equivalent of 50% to 75% of their annual income from their primary job, they can then quit and work on their recruitment business full time.

The thinking here is that if you can earn 50% of your annual income working a couple of evenings per week, when you are able to devote more time to your agency, then your income will skyrocket.

She said that she does not have the time to do this as she is busy working on her MLM business.

I said, how's that going? Not bad was her reply, but I am not making any money.

Now, she should definitely be wanting to throw in her cards with that business model.

On average, 99% of all MLM distributors in these network marketing companies earn less than £10.00 a week in commission income and spend hours recruiting for those at the top to get filthy rich.

In fact, we do have a referral programme that pays £500 for each successful introduction.

Not only that, but we also provide you with all the tools, products and training, so it's more than a side hustle.

No, starting a home-based recruitment agency is a real business, most definitely worth the risk.

The masterclass training programme will provide you with all the skills and knowledge required to set up and run a successful home-based recruitment agency.

Outlined below are just a sample of some of the subjects that will be covered in the programme:

- Introduction to starting a recruitment agency
- How to set up your recruitment agency to run on a shoestring budget
- How to obtain immediate vacancies for your business
- How to find and interview qualified candidates

- How to conduct business with employers and their hiring managers
- What exactly to say to employers and candidates to help manage every step of the recruitment and hiring process
- How to coordinate job interviews by telephone and prepare candidates for their interviews
- What fees to charge and how best to present the cost-effectiveness of your service
- How to participate in salary negotiation and handle potential 'deal breakers.'
- How to make a placement in 30 days or less
- How to establish an enviable database of candidates.

Unlike most network marketing programmes, our recruitment start is a business definitely a *card hand* worth keeping.

Starting your very own home-based recruitment agency gives you the freedom and flexibility to set your schedule, sales objectives, and realistic targets.

And this book can be your first step to having your share of this very lucrative multi-billion-pound industry.

The next step will be to attend my free recruitment start-up online event at www.recruitmentagencyrevolution.com/join, where you can find out more about this business opportunity and also where you can book a 45-minute call with me directly so that I can answer any questions you may have about getting started.

The song concludes with the words, ***"Cause every hand's a winner, and every hand's a loser."***

This points to the need for you to understand your market, your industry, and your products.

When you are a lone business owner working by yourself to grow your business, things can be challenging.

It's not that it's hard to get started; that's something most people can do when they put their minds to it.

What's hard is knowing what to do to help grow your business.

This is what many people who start a business have trouble with and what causes a number of small businesses to throw in the towel before they really have a chance to get anywhere.

There are several reasons why businesses don't grow, and it is not always financial.

More often than not, it boils down to not having the expertise to do all the business requirements; hiring the right experts can save both you and your business.

You can't do it all alone, no matter how knowledgeable or capable you might be.

No man is an island, and that is true in the business world! No one is self-sufficient; everyone relies on others for something.

There will be some things you can do well and to a high standard in your business and enjoy doing.

However, there will be other elements of running a business where you lack the know-how and may not be something that can simply be ignored.

The perfect answer is to find someone who can do what you can't or who can do it better than you can; this will free up your own time to do more of what you are good at.

CHAPTER 1

Reasons Why You Should Start Your Own Home-Based Recruitment Agency

My goal in offering this business opportunity is to start a recruitment agency revolution by giving ordinary people from all backgrounds, education, and walks of life, yes YOU, the chance to run your very own online home-based recruitment agency, which for far too long has been the preserve of the rich and privileged.

Now people are interested in starting their own businesses for many different personal reasons.

However, in the overwhelming majority of cases, they, and quite possibly you, have one or more of the following reasons in common for wanting to do so:

- You are tired of working relentlessly only to line your employers' pockets without any real appreciation for your efforts.
- No matter what you do, you just cannot seem to earn enough money to make ends meet.

- You are one of the tens of thousands of people who are now on zero contract hours with no guarantee of regular work, just at the beck and call of your line manager and worse still at very short notice or even no notice at all.

- The only way you can make more money is to do even more overtime when you can get it, and which is then taxed to the hilt!

- Worse still, your boss has taken liberties asking you to work longer hours additional shifts with no extra pay because of the economy.

- You haven't had a pay increase for a number of years, and because of the rise in the cost of living, you have very little disposable income.

- You have no retirement pension or savings, and you're having a hard time paying the bills.

- Your family life is suffering because you are unhappy with your financial status and now taking medication just to help you get through the day.

- You were one of the three million excluded for over a year from any government support during the pandemic, and now you're struggling to keep your head above water.
- You have come to realise that there is no such thing as "job security" anymore and that the only person who can do anything about your financial future and independence is you. Yes, YOU.
- And finally, you HATE feeling like your life is being controlled by other people or circumstances beyond your control – and there is an urgent need to get your life back, TAKE CONTROL, take action, right now, once and for all.

Do any of these set of circumstances match how you feel or where you are at this point in time?

Would you agree that it's high time you did something about it and change your life for the better?

Well, now you can!

If you have been looking for a lasting solution to any of these problems, you can stop chasing those shiny objects; the so-called get-rich-quick schemes that frankly do not exist.

This book will put you on a course to learning how you can break free from your 9 to 5 existence and gain real financial freedom.

You can start your recruitment agency on a part-time basis and quickly learn how to start earning good money in a few short weeks.

I am talking in terms of earning, on average, £4,000 to £6,000 by just placing one candidate into a job.

Would earning an extra £6,000 per month be of benefit to you in your current situation?

Just think for a moment or two what a positive impact earning that level of income would have on your life today.

If where you are at now is not where you want to be, then today, you have the opportunity to decide to take your first step on the road to gaining a lifestyle most people can only dream about.

If you haven't done so already, please book now to attend a free online presentation, where you can book a

45-minute call with me directly to discuss in greater detail what you need to do to get up and running.

www.recruitmentagencyrevolution.com/join

Over the last decade or so, the recruitment industry has been one of the fastest-growing businesses in the UK, doubling every five years or so.

Recruitment is still one of the only few industries that require a relatively small investment. It can be run on a shoestring budget. There is minimal official regulation and can equally yield tremendous financial results in a very short period.

In many respects, running a home-based recruitment agency has one of the lowest barriers of entry to the highest level of income.

In addition to this, the opportunities within the recruitment industry are unlimited, for example:

- You will never run out of candidates looking for jobs or even wanting to move to a better job.
- You can select any niche market or area of specialisation. It gives you the flexibility to work within an industry that you have knowledge of

or choose a specific market that you have a personal interest or desire to work in.

- You will never run out of prospects to develop into clients.

In a recent report by the Recruitment Employment Confederation, they stated:

"The jobs market continues to go from strength to strength with a further increase in the number of people finding new jobs."

- The service you provide is greatly needed. When a client advertises a position, they are inundated with candidates that can take an age to sift through. This process is extremely labour intensive and not very cost-effective at that as there are no guarantees of a successful outcome.

The staffing and recruiting business is here to stay. It has been around since the time of Julius Caesar. He promised a reward of 300 sestertii to any soldier who brought another to join the Roman army.

Interestingly the amount represented a third of a soldier's annual salary. Coincidently on par with the fees charged by recruitment agencies today - 30% of the candidates' annual salary. We will elaborate more on this topic later.

- This is an extremely rewarding business — where else can you change people's lives for the better on a regular basis? If you are unemployed or have ever been unemployed, it can be a very dark and lonely place to be. However, when you help someone find a job, you bring a ray of sunshine into their lives, which is extremely satisfying.

And finally, when you have your own recruitment agency you have lifelong income and job security...

...and you never have to worry about working for a company that is in the process of "cutting back," "downsizing," "laying off," "restructuring," "re-engineering," "streamlining," "re-balancing," "furloughing," and the new buzz word, "rightsizing." Whatever that means.

Once upon a time, layoffs were an oddity. Today they are the norm, but not if you have your own business.

CHAPTER 2

How My Experience and Expertise Will Help You To Succeed

Just before I launch into the meat of the training, I would like to briefly outline a bit about my back story, which will hopefully give you the confidence to join the 90 days recruitment programme.

I've worked in the recruitment industry for some 40 years.

During my time in recruitment, I have worked at Director, and Senior Management level for companies such as Reed Employment, Blue Arrow, Crown Personnel, and DP Connect, to name a few.

This is a picture of me working for a well-known UK recruitment agency called Reed Employment, hosting a charity event to help raise funds for the National Children's Home, with the late British actor Bill Owen from the BBC sitcom 'Last of the summer wine.' Some may recognise him.

I know what you're thinking; you're looking at my picture and saying to yourself, isn't time cruel.

Well, it was over 30 years ago.

Ok, moving swiftly on.

I have written a number of books relating to various aspects of the recruitment industry such as 'How To Start A Career In Recruitment,' 'How To Find Your Ideal Job In The Shortest Time Possible,' 'Recruitment Secrets Revealed,' plus articles and reports for the recruitment industry.

All these books are in the resource library as part of my masterclass training programme. The information contained in these publications is very informative.

I've been a panel expert for 'Start Your Business' magazine, where I provide answers to questions and advice to budding entrepreneurs regarding recruitment and starting a business.

Over the past five years, I have been a keynote speaker at the Business Start-Up Show in London, where I have presented to hundreds of people the benefits of starting a home-based recruitment agency.

I am a fellow member of the Recruitment and Employment Confederation (REC), the highest level of membership for the organisation, which is effectively the governing body for the recruitment industry here in the UK.

I have personally secured several multimillion-pound contracts during my time in recruitment, with companies such as:

Guy's and St Thomas Hospital, Price Water House Coopers, London Ambulance Service, IBM, PWC,

National Grid, Royal mail, Barclay's bank, Unilever, Department of Health, The Home Office, to name a few.

I also had one more notable contract to supply temporary staff to the Royal Household of Buckingham Palace.

I will cover that experience in the next chapter.

Most importantly, with this experience and expertise, to date, my company has helped hundreds of ordinary people to learn how to gain real financial freedom by setting up their very own home-based recruitment agency.

CHAPTER 3

Supplying Staff To Buckingham Palace

I would just like to relate a very brief experience, if I may, which highlights how fascinatingly interesting this business can be.

On a very sad occasion, the recruitment branch I was managing in Victoria, London, won the contract to supply staff to Buckingham Palace to sort through letters of condolences when Princess Diana was killed in a car crash back in 1997.

Buckingham Palace has its own post office called the 'Court Post Office' staffed by a small team called the 'Royal Postmen.'

The Queen reportedly receives around 300 letters per day; however, even with having her own post office, they were completely overwhelmed by literally thousands of letters and cards of condolences for Princess Diana.

Now Buckingham Palace does not use the traditional Royal Mail postal vans.

When the post arrives, they have horse-drawn carriages to take the mail from Buckingham Palace to Kensington and then onto St James Palace.

As you can imagine, because of the share volume of sacks of mail being redistributed in these relatively small carriages, it took an age for the temps to get through all the incoming posts.

On one occasion, I had to get the timesheets signed off for all the temps working at the St James Palace location so that they could be paid, but there was no one available.

So, in my 'infinite wisdom', *(not),* I thought, I would just go and search around inside the palace to find someone to sign off the timesheets (*and of course, it had nothing to do with me wanting to have a little nose around to see how the other half lives*).

St James Palace is not open to the public for tours unless you have been invited as a guest as it is occupied by members of the royal family. Therefore, searching inside the palace for someone to get a signature for the timesheets wasn't a very good idea.

After a few minutes of casually strolling around, admiring the artwork, plush red furniture and carpets, plus gold-gilded décor, I heard a voice from behind saying, ‘can I help you?’

So, I spun around, and there was a very elegant-looking lady standing there with a quizzical look on her face. Sometimes know when you recognise a face, but you can’t quite remember where you have seen them before or even their name.

So, I said to her, ‘I know you, where do I know you from?’

One of the security guards confirmed my suspicions that she was Princess Michael of Kent, or to give her the correct title, HRH Princess Michael of Kent, that I had bumped into.

Talk about me being dumb and dumber for not recognising her, and it gets worse.

She continued... *‘Yes, but I don’t know you! So, what are you doing in the palace?’*

Oh, I do apologise, I said, but I am from the recruitment agency, and we have a team of temps working and sorting out the letters and cards of condolences.

Oh, Ok, that's fine. So, I thought, phew, she's not going to send for the palace guards and get me turfed out or worse still arrested and thrown into the London dungeons.

She then asked how it was going?

It was on the tip of my tongue to say that there is light at the end of the tunnel, but under the circumstances of how Princess Diana was fatally injured, that would definitely not have been a good response.

So, trying to think quickly for an alternative answer, I said we are coming to the end of the lollipop. (I know, I did say it gets worse).

Lollipop, lollipop, she replied; why are your temps eating lollipops? They're going to ruin the cards.

To my shame, I replied, I am not too sure why, but I better go and sort them out.

Not one of my better days in the office, especially as I forgot to ask her to sign the timesheets, but certainly memorable for all the wrong reasons.

On this assignment, we had hundreds of temporary workers that were paid hourly rates.

Today, many businesses with high-traffic seasons or cyclical work schedules are looking for temp agencies to outsource short-term jobs and projects to knowledgeable individuals looking for work.

Recruitment agencies provide businesses with workers on a case-by-case basis to perform the necessary tasks at the business's most crucial times.

They also provide a cost-efficient way for companies to conduct business without having to hire full-time employees.

Due to the nature of their work, most hire workers in health care, accounting, technical jobs, or project manager roles.

Several recruitment agencies now recruit people onto their books for roles such as substitute teachers and day labourers specifically for their long-term assignments.

Recruitment agencies, by and large, have their finances structured in such a way that the revenue generated from the temporary side of the business fully covers all the running costs of the company, with the permanent revenue set aside as the profit.

Operating this way ensures that they will be able to meet all their running cost by the regular income from temp contracts.

Our Recruitment Agency Revolution masterclass coaching programme provides in-depth training on how to target and successfully tender for large temporary contracts.

This is an area that I have a wealth of experience, and I would love to share it with you if you decide to come on board.

CHAPTER 4

Choosing An Industry To Start Your Recruitment Agency

It is safe to say that all sectors of the UK economy over the last year or so have been impacted by the global pandemic, with some sectors such as retail being irreversibly affected.

However, there are a number of industries that are proving extremely resilient and are set for tremendous growth; these are as follows:

Construction Industry

To start with, the sector breaking the most records is the construction industry.

Construction often involves short-term projects and tight deadlines; recruitment agencies are crucial in sourcing contractors in such situations, especially on large-scale projects and at a technical or executive level.

These construction firms choose to search for potential employees with the help of recruitment agencies who know both the sector intimately and the needs of particular roles and positions within the industry.

Information Technology

With sustained year-on-year growth in total vacancies, greater clusters of tech companies emerging in pockets across the UK, and optimism exuding from all corners of the sector, it's fair to say that those in the IT industry are feeling rather bullish about the future.

London remains the nation's leading tech cluster, but with several other peripheral cities driving their own start-up ecosystems, that mantle may well not stay with the capital for too much longer.

With the vast majority of tech companies forecasting growth this year, the sector's optimism is high, with new investment in infrastructure being made to support greater volume.

Care Industry

The care industry is rapidly expanding too. This is mainly due to the growth in the number of mature individuals who want to stay in their own homes but may need help with their daily tasks.

This sort of work can prove to be very rewarding, but a good work ethic is essential, as well as a fair degree of patience.

Oil & Gas / Energy

Despite constant warnings that we are 'only 30 years away from running out of oil,' and fluctuating oil prices, demand continues to grow.

Add to this the boom in other energy areas such as shale gas extraction, along with green energy programmes, and you have a market primed for recruiters.

The oil and gas sector needs to recruit tens of thousands of new employees worldwide over the next decade to avoid skills shortage, according to PricewaterhouseCoopers research, and companies in the sector are pushing hard to attract employees into this interesting and exciting, not to mention a well-remunerated industry.

Service Sector

In addition to this, the services sector, which embraces everything from restaurants and pubs to law firms and estate agents, is also seeing a rapid expansion of output, new orders and, of course, employment, especially as we emerge from the lockdown.

CHAPTER 5

Why Employers Use Recruitment Agencies

The most common reason, particular for lower-level jobs, is simply to save time and effort.

Many organisations don't have the staff to sift through all the CVs generated by an advert in a newspaper or on the internet, so they use a recruitment agency to bring the numbers down to a more manageable level.

In fact, it is not unusual for a client to receive hundreds of CVs for one post, with the vast majority of these CVs totally unsuitable for the role.

Then there are endless enquiries several weeks after the position has been filled.

When I was working for a recruitment agency in central London, PricewaterhouseCoopers PWC was looking for an office manager. They made the mistake of advertising the post in a local newspaper, and they were inundated with candidates, as you can well imagine.

They decided to short cut the whole process and offer the position to an internal candidate.

One applicant who had submitted her CV wanted to know in writing why she was not selected.

The HR department kindly responded, informing her that they had opted for an internal employee who had applied for the post.

The lady was not happy with the response from PWC and demanded to see the CV of the employee who got the job because she believed that she was a more suitable candidate. Can you believe that?

Well, never in a million years were PWC going to do that. So, after a few months of letters going to and fro between the two parties, the candidate became so indignant that she got a sleeping bag and camped outside the offices of PWC in protest.

Of course, that is a little extreme, but it illustrates the point.

Conversely, if the company only recruits on an ad hoc basis, perhaps just a couple of times a year, it is certainly not cost-effective to have a paid employee in an HR role to handle their recruitment.

Many clients realise, after dabbling with trying to save money by doing the recruiting themselves, that it is more cost-effective to use the services of a recruitment agency, primarily for the following reasons:

- Recruiters have access to a pool of interviewed, reference and skills tested candidates whose CV can be forwarded to clients at short notice. Some candidates are hard to find. They may be passive or selective and not keen to have their CV on a job board.
- Even if a candidate is not currently actively looking for a new job, there's a strong chance that a good recruiter will know who they are and how to reach them.
- Agencies have many networks. Each consultant, candidate, client, or head-hunter has the potential to leverage their networks to help connect to people with a range of skills and experiences. Many of whom would be off the radar of an in-house team or hiring manager.
- Recruiters define and describe the position best. The use of a recruitment agency will help clients to focus on precisely what they are looking for.

- A recruiter knows what talent is available and can provide guidance on sourcing a suitable candidate for the position they are trying to fill, the availability of talent, and the going rate or salary required to pay to attract the best talent.
- Recruiters save employers time and cost. A search for an employee distracts line managers and will also cost the company more money than a vacancy turned over to a recruitment agency.

It's all about helping the client to value their employee's time. Advertising fees, staff salaries, interview overheads, taking up references, liaising with the candidate, supplies, technology, and other expenses are all part of the hiring process's costs.

With their pool of screened and interviewed candidates unknown to the clients, recruitment agencies save employers the effort and costs of investing in an HR department.

Increased Reach – Passive Candidates

A vast network and multiple hiring tools mean recruitment consultants can be more effective and efficient in finding suitable candidates.

Recruitment agencies spend money to utilise multiple tools in sourcing candidates for vacancies.

Outlined below are some of the measures they take to build a strong database of candidates:

- Advertising in trade magazines and newspapers
- Targeted local newspaper advertising
- Open days and job fairs
- Use of candidates already registered with the agency
- Referrals from candidates already registered
- Competitions and incentives to attract candidates, such as refer-a-friend

They have decades of experience in their field and know where and how to look, whilst also having clear links to a vast network full of potential candidates.

This also means access to all of the best 'passive' candidates for any given industry. Those who a company would otherwise miss out on because they are not actively looking or applying for jobs.

Quality 'candidates' over applicants

As previously mentioned, recruitment agencies have access to 'passive' candidates, those who are not applying or actively seeking a new job.

These are usually the best candidates. Many of a company's efforts and budget when hiring for a role can be spent on attracting applicants through advertising. The vast majority of these applicants will not be a good fit for the organisation.

This is not an issue for the recruitment agency, as these surplus candidates will just be added to their database, as they may be suitable for other vacancies that they have on their books.

Using a recruitment agency grants access to candidates that are more suited to a vacancy. They can do all the vetting of candidates that are a perfect match in terms of skills and overall suitability for the role.

As experts in hiring and interviewing in their field, a recruitment agency can understand a candidate's skill set and identify where they would fit in naturally.

The agencies experience also gives them more control. Recruitment consultants will manage the candidate from the initial stage of CV screening through to ensuring the candidate arrives on time for their first day.

This means clients don't have to deal with all the organisational headaches of managing multiple applicants.

Ears to the ground

The best recruitment agencies will have decades of knowledge in their market. Working in partnership with a company's HR team, the consultants can be their eyes and ears in the market.

With a wealth of knowledge in their industry, an understanding of salary expectations, where and how to find available talent and career expectations, recruitment consultants have a lot to offer in supporting the hiring process.

This knowledge and experience also allow them to tackle any challenges in hiring candidates required at short notice.

Nothing to lose!

Ultimately, an employer has nothing to lose. They don't pay anything upfront, and the best agencies offer good rebate terms. So, if the candidate who is placed isn't the right fit, companies are given a free replacement or partial refund of the fee paid.

Temporary Assignments

Let us now turn our attention to the reasons why employers use an agency for temporary staff cover

Nowadays, you find that the vast majority of companies turn to recruitment agencies to supply them with temporary staff that can be quickly deployed to cope with unforeseen demand, special one-off projects, cover sickness, holiday absence and maternity leave.

Plus, to provide extra support due to seasonal peaks like the festive seasons, end of year sales, etc.

The use of temporary staff can also reduce the fixed costs associated with labour hiring and recruitment.

Temporary workers, for example, represent a relatively low-cost method of screening for potential permanent employees, monitoring their job performance and suitability.

Recruiting permanent staff from a pool of temporary workers enables employers to 'try them out for size' over a longer period than would be possible under most probation schemes.

Instead of paying ridiculously high prices just to circulate adverts through newspapers, television and other forms of media to source for candidates, companies can merely pay the services of their chosen recruitment agency to get the best-qualified employees they need within a day or two.

This ensures that they don't have to spend more time and money on human resources to filter the numerous CVs they receive.

If you put the costs companies pay for adverts and human resources, not to mention the untold man-hours sifting through the CVs against the fee paid to a recruitment agency, informed companies who have done the math could see just how much money they will be saving.

Another reason for using the services of a recruitment agency is when the position is a very senior or highly specialised one. In this case, the employer appoints an executive search agency that specialises in 'headhunting' to find people for that particular profession or level of experience, with good contacts in that field.

However, the overriding reasons why a company would use a recruitment agency is because:

1) They cannot quickly find suitably qualified candidates for their vacancies. In the vast number of cases, the candidates are registered with the recruitment agencies in the first place and rely on the agency to find suitable jobs for them.

2) In some instances, clients are looking to recruit a person who is not necessarily actively looking for a job, and they will need first of all to be sourced or headhunted and then enticed into considering an alternative position, perhaps with more money or better prospects.

It's unethical for clients to directly poach or approach candidates working for a competitor, but they can employ the services of a head-hunter or an executive search consultancy to 'sound' out a person to see if they might be interested in a move.

3) when they have a rush job, a one-off project or unforeseen extra workload and they need to get several people in at short notice.

In fact, more and more recruitment agencies are resorting to a sneaky little tactic of discouraging candidates from applying directly to a client's advertisements, whether on their website or in a newspaper advertisement.

This is what the recruitment agency will say to the candidate "if you see a vacancy either on a company's website or in a newspaper advert, there is no need for you to approach the client directly, all you will simply need to do is to provide me with the details of the vacancy, and I will approach the client on your behalf.

This will, of course, increase your chances of getting the job exponentially, as having someone vouching for you as a third party will enable you to steal a march on other candidates.

Plus, the recruitment business is quite incestuous, and because every day I am constantly on the phone talking to companies, I will probably have dealt with or even personally know this client.

To the candidate, all this makes perfect sense. Of course, the main reason why the agency is offering this service is because of the placement fee that they will be charging the client if this candidate is taken on by the employer, even though the candidate has done half the work by giving the job to the agency.

What candidates are not aware of, though, more often than not, the agency does not always forward their CV to the company in the first instance, even though they have referred the vacancy to the agency.

Why?

Well, if that candidate's CV is not strong enough or they have a more suitable candidate on their database, as is often the case, then a candidate from their existing database will be forwarded to the company first.

Why?

Again, because they are in the business of making money. Is that a little naughty? I would say so, but sadly it happens on a fairly regular basis.

The third reason is confidentiality. The employer may be a high-profile organisation that wants to avoid the publicity involved in an advertisement or to avoid unsuitable applicants who are attracted by the name and not necessarily the job role.

Can you imagine how many applicants Elon Musk would get for a marketing manager for SpaceX?

Or a company may be seeking to replace someone who won't know they're being replaced until their line manager turns up with an empty box for them to clear their desk.

Ouch!

CHAPTER 6

Why Now Is The Perfect Time To Start A Recruitment Agency

Twenty years ago, was an entirely different world for a recruiter. The high street recruitment agencies had the industry pretty much sown up.

The cost of setting up a recruitment agency was extremely expensive, which prevented hordes of competition in the space and, as a result, recruiters could retain and form lasting relationships with clients a great deal easier than it is today.

This was despite high recruitment fees and, on occasion, lacklustre performance on the part of the agency both towards the candidates and, surprisingly, the clients.

Having a prime high street location that attracted candidates drawn in from adverts in their window display or an A-board outside their offices enabled agencies to develop an extensive database of candidates, which was the best way to generate vast sums of placement fees from employers.

The majority of clients didn't expect dozens of applicants for each open job from the agency; sometimes, just two or three candidates' CVs would suffice.

Job seekers would come to the recruiter's office to see the vacancies advertised in the window display and then call in to register.

Fax machines were the preferred method of CV submission; still, snail mail also provided a great outlet.

Fewer job seekers meant applicants and recruiters enjoyed a more personalised relationship with one another, with the recruitment agencies, by and large, calling all the shots.

Over the next two decades, the internet would profoundly affect the recruitment industry and would present untold opportunities for savvy business entrepreneurs to set up a home-based recruitment agency.

Let me illustrate why this is the case.

We have seen quite a few large high street retailers go to the wall during the past few years.

As we know, this has primarily been due to the widespread use of the internet that has made it possible for people to buy products and services online at a reduced price.

As a spin-off, it has also given ordinary people a unique opportunity to set up a business from home, providing candidates to the company's vacancies at a fraction of the price of costly bricks and mortar businesses.

As alluded to earlier, high street recruitment agencies are certainly not immune to the challenges of the internet.

The majority of high street recruitment agencies are acutely aware that the whole industry had shifted online, and having a £100k to £150k per year prime piece of real estate that served a by-gone era when people used to come in off the street to register for jobs is now like having a millstone tied around their necks.

And unfortunately, although it is crippling their business, they are locked into very costly and lengthy leases, some 15, 20, 25 years or more, making it nigh impossible for them to quickly downsize or reinvent themselves and move with the times.

It's interesting to note that a recent analysis of high-street openings and closures in the UK showed that recruitment agencies had one of the highest closure rates in Britain's town centres for retailers with multiple branches.

These closures are a sign of the decreasing importance of operating from a high-street location. The increased use of social media, e-commerce and changing client and candidate needs are the key reasons for the decline.

High street recruitment agencies' operating costs, running what is effectively a retail shop business, are extremely expensive.

As previously stated, they have high rents, high services charges, high rates, high head office cost, high maintenance and security cost, high insurance fees, high staff wages; the list is endless.

Therefore, it is nigh impossible for them to reduce the fees they charge to employers.

You may or may not be aware that many recruitment agencies are still charging employers a whopping 30% of a candidate's annual salary as a finder's fee.

Yes, almost a third of the candidate's annual salary. On average, here in the UK, it's £8,000 to £10,000 for each candidate they place into a job.

And believe it or not, for a retained search assignment for a more senior position or difficult to fill roles, clients can be charged up to 50% as a fee, which can equate to the price of a new car!

Now the current economic climate has made every company, both large and small, think long and hard of ways in which they can reduce their overheads.

Top of their agenda is finding and utilising a more cost-effective recruitment service instead of paying the exorbitant costly fees charged by traditional high street recruitment agencies.

This, coupled with the explosive growth of the e-commerce industry and the easy accessibility of new e-recruitment tools such as job boards, social media platforms, CV databases, and Applicant Tracking Systems, has made it affordable for people to join the industry.

This has created a golden opportunity where you can quickly and easily learn the skills and knowledge required to set up your own home-based recruitment agency.

I will prove how easy it is to make money as a recruiter; better than that, I am going to show you how you can gain access to all the products and services needed to get started.

Our unique recruitment start-up business model based on my 40 years of recruitment experience coupled with the knowledge gained from helping hundreds of new start-ups has been specifically designed for you to simply find vacancies and forward suitable CVs to companies looking to fill these positions.

However, instead of charging 30%, you will be offering a more realistic fee structure of 10% or charging a flat fee, undercutting high street agencies, winning and gaining repeat business.

To find out more about the services we offer in terms of helping you to set up your very own home-based recruitment agency, simply register to attend either my recruitment start-up online presentation, where you can also book an appointment to discuss how to get started at the end of this event.

www.recruitmentagencyrevolution.com/join

Operating a home-based recruitment agency that generates high-profit margins, even after reducing your fees to clients, coupled with minimal overheads and low running costs, allows your home-based recruitment agency to undercut and take business from even well-established recruitment companies who, because of their high overheads, are powerless to compete.

We will cover more on exactly how this works in practice shortly...

One thing I can assure you is that there has never been a better time to start your own home-based recruitment agency because you are ahead of the curve, and this is where you can quite simply be the iTunes of the recruitment industry.

Rest assured that this business model works, and there is absolutely no reason why it cannot work for you too.

CHAPTER 7

The Benefits Of Starting A Home-Based Recruitment Agency

Low Overheads

A home-based recruitment business costs relatively little to set up, and you don't have to worry about rent, rates, and all the other expenses associated with business premises.

The lower your expenses, the more profit you get to keep, and the easier it is to manage your cash flow.

Working from a home-based office keeps your overheads low as you are not renting office space or paying for any office utilities.

The zero commute also saves money on petrol and wear and tear on your car.

The reduction in fixed costs allows you to be more flexible in your pricing decisions than your competitors, who must cover those types of expenses.

You can choose to either give more favourable quotes with your fees and, in some cases, even get away with keeping the same pricing as your competition and have a healthier bottom line.

Save Time

You eliminate the time it takes to commute to and from your workplace when you work from home. This could easily amount to 8-10 hours a week, and that's equivalent to one whole working day saved every week!

One of our clients had this same experience of travelling three hours per day, 15 hours per week, 60 hours each month, and he said when you take into account that you don't get paid for travelling time, it is so disheartening.

He said Joe, now that I have started my home-based recruitment agency, I get up at 11 am every morning, and at five minutes past 11, I am at work.

You see, he has his laptop, computer and phone by his bed and wakes up and just reaches over, grabs his laptop, and starts work.

Now it goes without saying that this is not to be recommended.

You need to get up, get washed and get dressed to get in the right mindset for work. If you work from your bed

20 mins or so later, the sheets are going back over your shoulder, and your fast asleep — that's not a good practice to adopt.

Unlike the so-called get-rich schemes, this is not a business where you make money in your sleep. You have to work for it.

The only place success comes before work is in the dictionary.

You're the Boss

Answering to a boss is normal protocol when working a regular job, and having to report to a boss can sometimes be trying, to say the least.

I remember reporting to the owner of this recruitment agency, whose man-management skills left a lot to be desired.

He was the type of person that if you were on the edge of the precipice and needed his help, his advice would be to *put your best foot forward*.

Starting a home-based business allows you to be the captain of your own ship and takes away much of the stress of working in a regular job.

When you're the boss, although you'll still have deadlines and obligations to meet, you're the only person you'll have to answer to.

Your home-based recruitment agency does not involve overly demanding clients and customers as you can choose who you want to do business with, so you typically do not have to worry about them bossing you around either or being overly demanding.

With a successful recruitment agency, your money-making potential as the owner is often significantly higher than working for someone else.

Let's face it; all the most successful people in the world are their own bosses. As a successful business owner, no boss means no office politics, no petty rules, no asking permission to visit the dentist, or having to request in writing when you want to take your annual leave, etc. You have the freedom to work on your terms.

Flexible Working Hours

When you're the owner of a typical home-based recruitment agency, you can enjoy the flexibility of setting your own schedule. You can set your own hours and work when it's convenient for you.

This provides more free time for family activities or pursuing personal hobbies or interests. If you have school-age children, you'll never again miss helping your child's class with a day trip or project, and you'll never again have to turn down the chance to do something fun with your loved ones.

This business allows you to enjoy the freedom and flexibility you never thought you could afford.

Being your own boss allows you to work autonomously and independently by choosing your working hours.

You also have control of your business's direction as you develop and use your skills.

Break-even Quickly

Your break-even point is the point at which your turnover, minus your variable costs, equals your fixed costs, i.e., your business made neither a profit nor a loss. If you sell one more unit, then you're in profit.

Keeping overheads low means a more profitable business, and you'll be breaking even more quickly.

Typically, it can take up to two years for any high street business to break even. A number of companies go out of business during that time because of cash flow.

What is uniquely different about this business model is that your home-based recruitment agency can run on a 'shoestring' budget as everything is done over the internet. Therefore, with just one or two placements, you are in profit.

WOW!

Tax Advantages

Working from home allows you to offset certain household expenses against your profits, thus reducing your tax bill.

You can claim a percentage of the rent/mortgage, utilities, insurance and home maintenance, subject to the amount of space in your home that you have designated as a working area.

Tax deductions are one of the greatest benefits of running a home-based business. Keep receipts for everything purchased for use in your business.

From office equipment to the cost of heating and lighting the room where you work, it may all be tax-deductible.

Before you're ready to file your tax return, contact a financial advisor or an accountant regarding what items can be classed as tax-deductible.

Everything is Less Costly

Although, as previously mentioned, this business needs relatively little seed money to get started, there are still great bargains to be had for entrepreneurs who choose to set up to run their recruitment agency from a serviced office.

Everything is on the table for most companies to renegotiate terms; the pandemic's lasting effects have made negotiating for a low-cost service office a steal.

Again, in the masterclass training programme, we have a team in place who can negotiate those terms on your behalf.

When you are no longer tied to a time equal pound figure, the sky is the limit.

The difference is how hard you choose to work and how much time you can dedicate to working for yourself.

The end result is you making a much greater amount each day than you could if you worked for someone else in a job.

Therefore, in any respect, if you are prepared to, as the saying goes, *'Carpe diem,'* seize the day and truly go for it, you will find yourself on the verge of literally creating a business lifestyle that many people today can only dream about.

However, it is advisable that you don't give up your day job until you start seeing money rolling in.

The great thing about running a home-based business is that you can put as much or as little time into it as you like, always being mindful that the more time you do spend on your business, the quicker your business will grow into a successful and rewarding enterprise.

So, it's very easy for you to start on a part-time basis while still in employment, knowing that you have the choice of going full-time in your business when you feel it's justified.

Making money from home doesn't have to be an all-or-nothing situation.

But remember that in order to make a success of your company, it will eventually need your full-time attention.

When you stop and think about it, most people spend over 40 years of their lives working 40 weeks a year, and more than 40 hours a week, working to make someone else rich.

Does that make any sense to you?

When you take into consideration the points we have just covered, would you not agree that you are far, far better off working for yourself?

Absolutely!

Yet still, I can guarantee that the vast majority reading this book today, like the majority of people who attend our free recruitment start-up workshop presentations, will still prefer the so-called 'security' of a job.

That being said, the huge swath of people who are now coming to terms with the possibility of losing their job due to the pandemic has encouraged more to seriously look into starting a business of their own.

Studies have shown that only 15% or less of the world's population is capable of or have the opportunity of starting their own business – just 15%!

So, if you are reading this book, then you are likely part of that 15%, which is great.

Sadly, only 1%, maybe a little more, ever take action and start their own business; most people dream about starting a business but never take any action toward it.

A lot of people have been taught that running a business is risky and that the safe thing to do was to go out and get a job and have a career.

As previously mentioned, this is an outdated mode of thinking as many people have discovered over the past few years, to their dismay, that there is nothing safe about having a job.

These days very few people have any kind of job security as a company can cut you lose at any time.

And once a person has lost their source of income, they rarely have the finances to start anything in the way of a business, and if you end up on benefits, it's a struggle to pick yourself up from there.

I regularly meet people who are in this position, desperate to try and get out of their predicament; many had said they regret not starting their own business when they were working and had the finances to start something.

Now they are effectively at a dead end.

Some people love to say money isn't everything, but as the sales expert Zig Ziglar once said, it ranks right up there with oxygen. It's pretty important.

Life is short, and you don't want to go through life worrying about not having enough money to do the things you would like to do.

An increasing number of people realise that the real risk comes from actually not starting their own business, taking control, not at some distant time in the future but today, right now!

In the past, if you were made redundant a couple of times, it would be thought of as tough luck.

However, recent studies have shown that going forward, you're likely to be made redundant some six or seven times in your career. And each time you apply for a new job, it will be increasingly difficult to land one.

To add insult to injury, recent reports show that one in three UK jobs are at 'high risk' of being replaced in the future by, wait for it, robots.

With the lowest-paid workers most at risk of being replaced. Clerical and support roles are endangered, with a lot of this work being outsourced to companies employing low-paid workers in the Far East.

And if you think losing your job to a robot is a little farfetched, just speak to anyone who has previously worked on a production line in the motor industry.

Never forget the golden rule: *Whoever has the gold makes the rule!*

The thought that “having a corporate job is safe” is a thing of the past. Now, unless you are the person in charge, you are in jeopardy.

CHAPTER 8

How To Choose A User-Friendly Domain Name

When starting a recruitment business, one of the first things you need to do is choose a suitable name for your agency.

It is worth spending time considering the name since not only will this be the first thing potential customers see, but it will also be with you for the duration of your venture.

Choosing the name for your recruitment agency at first looks easy; you think of a name, canvass a few friends and colleagues, do a domain name search, and to your dismay, more often than not, that name has already been taken. So, it's back to the drawing board.

The first thing to keep in mind is to avoid choosing a name that may mean a lot to you, but that means 'diddly-squat' to your potential clients and candidates.

It is also worth avoiding names that are difficult to spell as potential clients will struggle to locate your website address.

Choosing a good domain name is crucial as your domain will usually be the first thing people see and hopefully remember.

The secret is for your name to be memorable and yet distinctive. Think about the nature of your business; can you boil that down to one or two words?

What is your company's Unique Selling Proposition (USP); if you are looking to specialise in providing, let's say, senior managers, you may want to create a name that denotes executive recruitment.

Every industry has certain protocols when it comes to naming.

For example, you wouldn't likely call your executive recruitment agency "Top Dog Services."

But you will have to decide on a name that reflects the nature of your business if you want to push the conventions of your sector in order to make your business name stand out.

Finally, it is good to try and hit on a name that is early in the alphabet and avoid numbers; people tend not to remember numbers or whether the numbers are spelt out.

Once again, you want to choose a name that is short, memorable, easy to spell, high up in the alphabet and preferably reflects the nature of your business, so much the better.

With regards to getting a website, we highly recommend a company called Blueprint Illustrated

www.blueprintillustrated.com

This company specialises in designing and developing attractive recruitment websites that not only look great but really add value to your business.

All of their websites are built to the latest web standards using modern techniques.

They function flawlessly and give start-ups a unique, engaging experience.

Websites are the backbone of modern business, and with today's web trends, using your website is a powerful tool to attract new clients and candidates.

This company can integrate your jobs and social media, helping to keep web content fresh and clients and candidates up to date.

Our recruitment start-up programme will provide you with a freely designed state-of-the-art recruitment website; all you will be required to pay is a nominal fee for the website's SEO and hosting.

CHAPTER 9

How To Make Money With Your Recruitment Agency – Finding Vacancies

It's incredible to think that as much as 85% of vacancies make up the hidden job market.

The truth of the matter is that it costs time and money to advertise a vacancy which can be very expensive.

And because an employer cannot guarantee that they will fill these positions, many will choose not to do so.

So, they place their jobs on their website, but unless the company is a household name, more times than not, these vacancies will just stay languishing on a client's website for months on end.

Although these vacancies do not get advertised externally, it is very easy for you to locate them.

So, let us go through ways in which you can access jobs that are part of the hidden job market.

Outlined here are a number of ways in which this can be done:

Social Media Sites - You can utilise sites such as Facebook, Twitter, and LinkedIn to network your way to find the contact details of hiring managers in your industry then check that individual company's website for vacancies.

Vacancies Listed in Your Local or National Newspapers - It is a good idea to create a 'scrapbook' to add these vacancies and call the company a week after they have placed their advert to see if they have had a good response.

If the vacancy has not been filled, then obviously you can offer your services. It is a good idea to offer the client a discount off your Terms of Business. Perhaps, even deducting from your fee the newspaper advert's cost, as long as it is not too expensive.

This way, the company doesn't feel that it has been double whammed, i.e., having to pay twice.

Type in the names of the top ten companies in your countries search engine followed by the word jobs, i.e., here in the UK, it is Google, so for example, you would type *'Amazon Jobs UK'* into the search engine, and there you will find hundreds of vacancies for this company.

Search the Leading Job Boards - Although most have vacancies from recruitment agencies, you will still find several direct vacancies from employers.

Family Referrals - Do you have a family member or a close friend who runs a business? Then ask them if they have any outstanding vacancies that you could help them with.

And don't just tap into the connections you already have.

Figure out who you need to know in your chosen industry to approach—likely the hiring manager—and make that connection, whether by getting them to follow you on Twitter by retweeting their tweets or growing your LinkedIn network until they become a third-degree connection.

Twitter, in particular, offers the opportunity to connect with professionals who might not otherwise give you the time of day.

Local Government Offices – Here, you would go to the local Town Hall, library, or contact your local council offices and make enquiries about any new companies relocating to your neck of the woods.

If they are relocating from some distance, then many of their existing staff won't necessarily be willing to relocate, which will result in open vacancies for you to fill.

It is best to contact the company before they relocate to your area; before they show up on your competitors' radar.

Most libraries and council offices have this information on their website, so make this your first port of call before going along directly to these places.

Chapter 10

How To Make Money With Your Recruitment Agency – Finding Suitable Candidates

Your next port of call is to find a suitable candidate.

Now there are numerous ways you can do this, and I would like to talk you through a few ways this can be done.

CV databases are a great way to gain access to millions of candidates from all sectors. It's quick and easy to search their database to find staff that match your roles.

If you would like advice and guidance on which is the best job board to use, simply contact any of my team, and they will be able to advise you on which one is best for your industry.

Recruitment Startup Consultancy is also able to secure highly competitive rates from these job board companies; my team can be contacted through our website **www.recruitmentstartupconsultancy.com**

There are dozens of job boards on the market, with an extensive database of millions of candidates offering a

CV search facility. It is best to use the services of a CV database within your niche market.

With the increasing numbers of CV databases coming on to the market, the cost of using these services is becoming ever more competitively priced, especially when compared with the money that can be generated from placing candidates from a Job board.

Facebook - Many people set up their own Facebook pages (separate to their profiles) that advertise the fact they're looking for a job.

There are also job-hunting groups you can look through, too, that will give you access to a great pool of potential candidates.

People tend to join these groups when they're actively looking for a job, so it's best to find ones tailored to the roles you're hiring for.

Look out for keywords in the group's name – such as 'recruitment' or 'sales' or 'business management,' etc.

Twitter - When people are job hunting, they tend to talk or tweet about it, so always search sites like Twitter for people who might be talking about their job hunt, plus you can follow people who might have jobs to offer.

Use Twitter Search to look for people who have tweeted relevant job offers in the past and follow them to see if it will happen again. Notice any keywords in common and then search on those too.

Also, watch how people reacted to those offers. Search more keywords to find conversations among other industry pros and follow them too.

LinkedIn - Works similarly to Facebook, in that you can track people who are job-hunting by browsing groups that have been named or tagged with job-hunting keywords.

Again, you'll need to target your search by keywords that specify the industry you're currently hiring for; it's no use looking in graduate groups if you want to recruit for the company director.

On LinkedIn, some people choose to link to their other profiles too, so if they have different social networks linked up on there, it might be worth taking note.

Sometimes (depending on the role), approaching someone via another network may work better.

Industry Meetups and Events - Depending on what industry you're hiring for, there may be a wealth of industry meetups, networking, and conferences happening in your town or city.

Use the website Meetup.Com to find them – and see if you can attend any yourself. It's a great way to meet people in person, and although not everyone will be looking for new roles or opportunities, they may not frown at the suggestion.

It's always worth asking – just in case they are and simply need a gentle nudge to do so. Nothing ventured, nothing gained.

These meetups will be full of influential industry folks, too, so be sure to do your research on who is going to be there and who you might expect to meet.

It makes such a huge difference than going in with no information or prior knowledge – and you'll look much more prepared and professional.

Student Websites and Forums - Students are always on the lookout for jobs and so make up a very large and enthusiastic bunch when it comes to candidates.
If you're hiring for a junior role or even a mid-level position, keep a graduate or student in mind for it.

There are plenty of online forums where students congregate and discuss job openings and job-hunting tactics.

Get involved on those forums and start building those relationships. Take a look at University websites, too, and find out whether they have any job-advertising space on their sites or if they have any internal student job search features.

If so, you could ask for a selection of candidates for a role you're currently hiring for.

Referrals - A tried and tested means of building your candidates' database is by asking every candidate you speak to within your niche industry if they know of anyone looking for employment and taking down their details.

It's a process where one contact leads to another, to another, and so on. All along the way, you collect contact details and CVs from potential candidates who may or may not fit the immediate job you are working on but seem worth keeping on file for future vacancies in your speciality area.

Prepare Your Search - Before you start your search; it is good first to identify the key skills required for the job and plan your search.

You want to use your time judiciously as it can be quite time-consuming sourcing CVs, so much so that most recruitment agencies have 'resourcers' on board specifically to do this task.

In our masterclass training programme, we will show you how this work can be outsourced overseas at a fraction of the cost of hiring staff.

If you just take the time to think, develop some semblance of a search strategy, and experiment with various searches, you can get to relevant results more quickly.

You should spend at least 5 -10 minutes thinking about and preparing your search strategy.

When you have successfully sourced a candidate before you send through the job specification to them, make sure you 'top and tail' the job spec by removing the company's name and, of course, your client's contact details.

Sadly, some candidates are pretty crafty and will contact the client directly and cut you out of the equation.

Do not over analyse CVs, as you could quite easily fall into the trap of analysis paralysis.

Firstly, the chances are that the people you are trying to find and recruit are not professional CV writers.

Whether they are software engineers, lawyers, physical therapists, project managers, or company directors – they are NOT an expert in CV writing, so they may not have included information relevant to the vacancy you're working on.

Worse still, some candidates have errors in their CVs that you may have to get them to amend before forwarding it to a client.

Some of the things people put on their CVs or cover letters are quite humorous.

I have picked out my top 10 favourite CV *faux pas* as examples of this:

1. "Nine-page cover letter accompanied by a four-page CV."

Here in the UK, there is a radio presenter named Nick Ferrari, who once worked with the media mogul Rupert Murdoch, and they were reviewing CVs for a graduates' post.

One of the applicants had a 13-page CV. Rupert Murdoch said I have been in the media industry for the past 50 years, and I have a one-page CV. This chap has been in the industry for less than a year, and he has a 13-page CV!

2. HOBBIES – "Space Travel."

3. MARITAL STATUS: - "Celibate."

4. OBJECTIVE: "One of the main things for me is, as the movie 'Jerry McGuire' puts it, 'Show me the money!'"

5. EMAIL ADDRESS – i-one-hotmale@hotmail.com and another one homeboy@hotmail.com

6. Reason for leaving: "I thought the world was coming to an end."

7. Let's meet, so you can 'ooh' and 'aah' over my experience."

8. Qualifications: "I have guts, drive, ambition and heart, which is probably more than a lot of the drones that you have working for you." (*Good one, insult all of this employer's staff; that's going to get you the interview. I don't think so.)*

9. A woman who sent her CV and cover letter without deleting someone else's editing, including such comments as "I don't think you want to say this about yourself here." *(I would have loved to have seen what she had written.)*

10. Finally, another reason for leaving – "After receiving advice from several different angles, I have decided to pursue a new line of work." Hmmm.

And again, because it's not every day a person goes for an interview, we have in our business pack a document with interview tips and techniques and a checklist that will significantly help improve your candidate's chances of getting the job.

It's true that job interviews can make even the most confident person nervous, but a little preparation can go a long way.

People make mistakes on an interview, but some errors are so over-the-top that they make the decision for a client not to hire them an easy one.

Sometimes candidates can let themselves down at the interview stage by doing or saying some crazy things that you just cannot prepare for. And again, I have picked out my top 10 of the most amusing.

1. One candidate, without asking, sipped the interviewer's tea.

2. Another one hugged the interviewer at the end of the interview.

3. The applicant refused to sit down and insisted on being interviewed standing up.

4. The candidate commented that he would do whatever it takes to get the job done, *legal or not!*

5. When asked why he wanted to leave his current employment, one candidate said that he had worked for his Mum for three years, but it is now time for a change!

6. When asked the question, where do you see yourself in five years, a graduate replied, “Student today. Vice president tomorrow!”

7. An interviewee was asked what person they would most like to meet, living or dead, and their response was the living one."

8. One interviewee mistook one of the female interviewers for a man! *Not good!*

9. When asked who the best person would be to contact for references, a candidate responded, ‘please do not contact my immediate supervisor at the company. My colleagues will give me a better reference.”

10. And finally, when an interviewee was asked why they left, they responded I would still be at the company if some muppet hadn’t snitched on me.

11. One more for good measure, one candidate filled out an application form with different colour crayons; you just wonder what planet some of these people are on.

Recruiters can also get it wrong with client visits. A bit of self-deprecation here; I visited a blue-chip client in central London one Friday, and the HR director that greeted me was wearing a smart corduroy suit.

I said, oh, I see you have a dress down Friday policy; she said no; why do you ask?

Ouch.

Needless to say, I did not win the business.

Coming back to sourcing a suitable CV. Candidates may not think to express every last bit of their experience in their CV – and if you're looking specifically for a key skill and it's not there, it's all too easy to assume that the person who wrote the CV doesn't have the requisite experience you're looking for.

Don't make assumptions about candidates from their CV.

There is no such thing as a CV that is a perfect match, so the best thing to do is to quickly scan through the CV and see if the candidate has the relevant key skills and experience required for the job.

And if you think the candidate is a good potential match, send them the job specification to look over and get back to you if they believe they are suitable for the position.

They will be the best person to judge if they are a suitable match for the vacancy.

The problem with most CVs is that sometimes the candidate is a very good fit for the job, but the skills and experience required for the vacancy are not explicitly expressed in their CV.

When selecting a suitable CV to forward to a client, it is not the case that one size fits all.

So, you will need to ask the potential candidate to completely rewrite their CV and tailor it to the job spec.

If they are interested in the position, they will not have a problem in doing so.

If they are not that keen or suitable, they will usually have an excuse why they cannot do it or will simply say 'can I get back to you,' but they seldom ever do.

But that's fine as the candidate is weeding themselves out and saving you the trouble.

In addition to rewriting and tailoring their CV so that it matches the job, they will also need to change their CV or cover letter profile.

Most CVs forwarded to clients miss the mark because they are not relevant to the job specification, and therefore, the client does not even give the CV a second glance.

The number one thing the client is looking for in a CV is to find a candidate that is a perfect fit for the position they are recruiting for.

Having just the relevant skills and experience is really a given. They are paying you a fee not just to get any old candidate, but to get the perfect candidate who can hit the ground running and pull up a chair, so to speak, and just get on with doing the job.

It is important that you send the candidate a registration form to complete giving you permission to forward their CV to prospective employers.

Chapter 11

How To Make Money With Your Recruitment Agency – Contacting The Client

The next step is to contact the client. This can be done in numerous ways, and I would now like to demonstrate how this is done.

Firstly, when directly contacting the client, the main obstacle you will face is getting past your contacts secretary, receptionist, or as they are sometimes known in the industry, the gatekeepers or rejectionists.

When you phone through, if you informed the receptionist that you are a recruitment agency, then you are dead in the water.

The response will be we don't use agencies; we have a preferred list of suppliers (PSL) in place that we stick to.

There will be a plethora of excuses why they will not put you through. So, try not to initially let on that you're phoning from a recruitment agency.

When phoning the company, simply say: "*Hi, my name is,* [and of course, give your name.] *I am interested in the vacancy your company has advertised for a project manager, can you put me through to* [the contact's name."]

Let me demonstrate this further, let's say the vacancy is for a Project Manager, and the line manager's name is Bob Stevens.

Your approach would be... *"Hi, my name is Joel Davis; I am interested in the vacancy you have advertised for a project manager; can you put me through to Bob Stevens, please. Thank you."*

The first thing to note is to end your request with the words 'thank you;' as you want this to come across as more of a command than a request.

When you say I am interested in the vacancy, you usually find the receptionist or PA will put you through at speed. Wait a minute, Mr Davis, I am sure Bobs around somewhere.

Why do you think this is the case?

Yes, they think you are the candidate. Are you interested in the position, yes, or no?

Well, if you answered yes, you would be right.

Of course, you are definitely interested in the position.

Now, if the receptionist misunderstands your level of interest, is that your problem?

So, they will invariably put you straight through.

When you're through to the client, you, of course, have to tell him that you are phoning from a recruitment agency. You can't try and pull the wool over his or her eyes by simply stating that you are 'interested in the job;' otherwise, you will just get short sharp shrift.

However, you don't have to reveal that you are phoning from a recruitment agency immediately.

The approach I would recommend is as follows:

"Hi Bob, my name is Joel Davis; I'm phoning in connection with your Project Manager vacancy; how convenient is it to talk? I need just two minutes of your time and no more."

At this point, you don't ask *is it convenient to talk* as he will simply say NO.

Therefore, simply ask *how convenient is it to talk*?

Now they cannot give a monosyllable, yes or no answer to a how type of question. Usually, they will ask what the call is about; or what is it concerning?

Now because he has not said that he does not have two minutes gives you a window to talk to him about a potential candidate.

Again, at this stage in the call, you still haven't fully disclosed that you are phoning from a recruitment agency.

Then you continue...

"The reason for my call is that I would like to put forward a candidate for your Project Manager vacancy.

Now I appreciate that you would want to see candidates who have directly responded to your advert. I fully understand that you may even have candidates to see; however, quality candidates with these skills are like gold dust, very hard to come by.

I can guarantee you that the candidate I would like to put forward for your vacancy is a perfect match for the position.

And what I would like to do is to send the CV across to you with my contact details, and if you are interested in the candidate, then all you will simply need to do is to call or email me back, and I will arrange a time for you to interview the candidate.

As a recruitment agency, we usually charge 30% of the candidate's salary as a fee; however, because it is the first time you will be using our service...

[or because you're a local health authority... or because we are just immerging from a recession.... or because of anything you care to choose that's appropriate]

...I will only be charging you a flat fee of just 10% of the candidate's annual salary, and of course, you only pay this fee if the candidate is as exceptional as I say they are, and you decide to take that person on to your payroll."

Now, what has the client got to lose in seeing your candidate's CV? Absolutely nothing.

In fact, the client would think that if this candidate is as good as you say they are, then they will indeed be saving thousands of pounds.

Just a word of caution here, when talking to the client about a potential candidate, you need to say to them that you *would like to put forward* a candidate and not that *you have a candidate* to put forward.

If you say you have a candidate, you run the risk of the client saying ok, tell me about your candidate, and if you haven't got one to hand, then you are in all kinds of trouble.

When you say *I would like to,* it is not the same as saying *I have*.

For example, a person saying that they *would like to own a yacht* is not the same as that *they have a yacht*; you get the point.

Another piece of advice, if you have a, pardon the expression, 'top draw' candidate that has everything the client is looking for and more, then you should aim to charge a fee of 20% and not 10%.

You may, from time to time, come up against a small independent recruitment agency that is working with a client on a Sole Supplier agreement, i.e., the client only uses that agency and has an agreement in place for a 10% placement fee.

If that is the case, there is nothing stopping you from reducing your fee to 7.5% or offering a straight flat monetary fee so that you can take up the mantle of their 'Sole Supplier.'

CHAPTER 12

WHAT CLIENTS ARE LOOKING FOR IN A CANDIDATE

Employers looking to recruit are tuned in to the radio station WII-FM *'What's In It For Me.'*

And therefore, your aim should be to forward a candidate with the 'Wow Factor.'

That is, when the client sees your candidate's CV, they go 'Wow!'

Let us consider two examples of what I mean by the expression 'Wow Factor'...

One of our new recruitment start-ups was looking for a Gemini 360 Software Operator, whatever that is. He did a CV database search and came up with five potential candidates.

The second person he spoke to said there's no need to talk to any other candidate as he is the perfect candidate for the job.

How so, said the recruiter; he replied that the software programme was his design, his invention, and then proceeded to rattle off a ten-digit patent certificate number for the software.

The recruiter then forwarded the CV along with a copy of the patent certificate as a Wow Factor.

The client sent back an email to say that he was on holiday but would be back in the office on Monday morning and that they could arrange for him to see the candidate on Monday at 11:00.

Did the candidate get the job? Most definitely, what better person to implement and train on the use of this software than the man who invented the programme?

Another one of our start-ups was recruiting for a Residential Care Home Manager.

They advertised the position online, and they were inundated with potential candidates.

They narrowed the search down by suitability and how close the applicants lived to the Care Home.

They then asked all the short-listed candidates to redo their CV by tailoring it to the job spec.

Plus, to modify their profile or cover letter as follows:

1. Show why they believe they are a perfect match for the job.

2. Their track record, proven ability, of working in a similar role. As they say in the game, 'past performance is indicative of future success.'

3. And last but not least, what they can bring to the table, in the way of a *'Wow Factor'* that is going to help the company make money, save money, or operate more effectively and efficiently so that they can make and or save money.

One of the candidates' profile stood out head and shoulders above the others.

This candidate's 'Wow Factor' was that she had recently been made redundant from her last job as a Residential Care Home Manager, and in many respects, she was a victim of her own success.

She had found and secured a lottery grant of £170,000 to add an extension to the Care home she was working at.

They also used some of the funds to refurbish the entire Care home with marble flooring, bi-folding doors that opened up, showing a beautiful panoramic view of the garden area and adding new furniture throughout.

She had the presence of mind to take a picture of the Care home before the work was started and the newly refurbished Care home.

As it was so attractive, people were transferring their elderly family members to this new Care home, so the revenue quadrupled.

To cut a long story short, the owner sold his Care home to a larger organisation that had its own Care Home Manager, and therefore, she lost her job.

But coming back to the aspect of her '*Wow Factor;*' she put on her CV a 'Wow Factor' that she knew exactly how to get hold of the grant funding for this Care home that she was applying for.

Do you think they would want to see her for an interview? I would say so.

Once the candidate has amended their CV, especially to include an irresistible Wow Factor, you then forward the CV to the client with an email saying:

"Hi Bob, further to our telephone conversation, please find attached the candidate's CV that I believe is perfect for your Project Manager vacancy.

Please, feel free to contact me on my telephone number here; alternatively, I will contact you in two days' time to see if you would like to know this candidate for an interview."

A word of caution here, sometimes you can fire off a CV and you poodle off to make a cup of tea, and the phone starts ringing, and you think who could that be, and when you answer the phone, it's the client.

You see, the problem is, in today's current job climate, skilled candidates are tough to come by and get snapped up quickly; therefore, when a client sees a suitable applicant, they tend to act fast.

When following up on the CV and contacting the client, you can again sidestep the receptionist by simply saying: *"Hi, my name is .... Please can you put me through to Bob Stevens please he is expecting my call;"* as per your email.

When you are through to your contact, you say: *"Hi Bob, it's* [give your full name], *from your* [agency's name.]

As promised, I sent through to you the CV of Stan Hughes for your Project Manager vacancy.

You would then highlight to the client the details of the candidate's profile 1) Why he is suitable for the role, 2) his track record of doing the job, and last but not least 3) his Wow Factor, what the candidate can bring to their business in the way of making money, saving money, or helping the client to operate more effectively, or efficiently to make money and or save money.

Now don't come up for air or test the client's understanding; simply go through the three points.

Then you say to the client, *"my candidate is available for an interview Wednesday afternoon or Friday morning; when would you like to see him?"*

You would, of course, need to double-check your candidate's availability.

Now here is the 64-million-dollar question: how do you know that the client is even interested in your candidate? You're trying to lock the client down with a *'half nelson'* move by asking *when* and not *if* he would like to see your candidate?

How do you know at this point in the conversation that he is definitely interested in seeing your candidate for an interview?

Yes, you've guessed it; he has not stopped you from talking to him about your candidate. If the client were not interested, they would have stopped you dead in your tracts.

The fact they haven't meant that they are interested in seeing your candidate, and it is usually the candidate's 'Wow Factor' that has piqued the client's interest.

The client tells you Friday afternoon; the next step is to prepare the candidate for the interview.

If possible, it is always best to meet the candidate before they go along for the interview, just to make sure they are who they say they are, and it would be advisable to check their employment credentials.

As you are working from home and do not have an office location, it is good to check out a local coffee shop with a warm, welcoming atmosphere and a place where you can conduct a discreet interview over a cup of coffee and a croissant.

Today, even well establish agencies conduct interviews this way as most candidates are conscious of going into or exiting an agency just in case they are seen doing so by a colleague or, worse still, their boss.

In the full training programme, we will go through how to conduct an interview and what proof of IDs you need to check.

Once you have vetted the candidate, you can arrange for them to meet the client.

Following the interview…

The client likes the candidate, usually because of the Wow Factor. The candidate likes the client; the client offers the candidate the job; the candidate accepts.

You then celebrate your first of many placements.

You then invoice the client, and you are paid a handsome fee, and then it's simply a case of wash, rinse and repeat.

This approach flat out works, and it will work for you too.

Now the vast majority of the well-established high street agencies do not spend as much time on their candidate's CVs; they adopt a spray and pray approach, sending dozens of CVs and simply playing the numbers game.

This is because each consultant is targeted to make three to four placements per week due to their company's costly overheads.

Your approach, though, is to *cherry-pick* one strong potential candidate for the job and then get the candidate to reformat their CV so that their CV mirrors the vacancy making them a perfect match for the vacancy.

This will inevitably lead to a higher success interview to placement ratio, which leads to more repeat business.

Now I've just shared with you a couple of my simple to implement, still, highly effective approaches to getting jobs, sourcing candidates, making a placement and generating £4,000 to £6,000 per successful introduction.

As previously stated, this information is not found anywhere on the internet or in any books.

However, those were just a couple of examples of the dozens of different techniques we cover in your step-by-step masterclass coaching and training programme.

Our latest business model requires no cold calling and has been designed to have clients queuing up to give you their business.

CHAPTER 13

The Way Forward

Now, if you want to start your very own home-based recruitment agency and found our new business model that is completely disrupting the recruitment industry, all you will simply need to do is attend one of my free recruitment revolutions online presentations. On the presentation, you will be able to book a 45-minute call for me to go through in detail how you can get up and running, in no time at all.

To find out the dates and times for these events, simply visit our website **www.RecruitmentAgencyRevolution.com/join,** or you can contact my team directly on 0800 622 6877 to book a place on my live workshop presentation.

Now again, please don't think that starting a recruitment agency is all going to be too much to handle, as our 'Done For You' business model has in-depth training videos, resource files, along with consultancy support to guide your every step of the way.

This is the exact business model that has helped our new recruitment companies to set up their agency and start earning a substantial income.

I would just like to add a disclaimer here.

It is very important that you understand that I am not guaranteeing any level of income, as a lot of your success will depend on how much time and effort you put into your business.

I'm going to share with you the steps you need to take to start making money; however, what you do with this information is entirely up to you to make it work.

Just A Final Recap On Why You Should Start Your Own Business Today

The benefits of Entrepreneurship are huge:

1. **You Have Greater Job Security**. Only a generation or two ago, going into business for yourself was considered risky, and the safest route was to get a good job in a large firm, perhaps a bank, retail, or working for the local council.

Now, working in a traditional job has become the risky option. Working for yourself has become the new job security.

If you're working for someone else, you're trading time for money and not building any real equity for yourself.

As the owner of your own recruitment agency, you immediately become the master of your own destiny.

If you think you will have job security working for someone else, think again...

2. **Freedom -** People love the benefits of working for themselves and enjoying the freedom they gain from designing their own prosperity.

You get to choose when you work, how you work and with whom you work. Best of all, you don't have to make the agonising choice between time for family and time for business.

With being your own boss, you will quickly see that you don't have to experience the world in the way you have been told.

3. **Flexibility -** It doesn't matter where in the world you live. Entrepreneurship is an equal opportunity employer.

E-mail, low-cost internet access and a new generation of recruitment tools make it possible to run a fully competitive recruitment agency from a home desktop.

Running a home-based business over the internet means you can expand your business to anywhere in the world. Wow!

4. **Make More Money -** There is a far greater opportunity to make money by building your own business than working for someone else. When you're in business for yourself, you write your own history; you write your own success story; you write your own legacy, and most importantly, you write your own paycheque.

To quote Paul Getty, one of the richest men of all time, he said, '*you can*

never get rich by working for someone else.' How true!

Being in business for yourself allows you to work your heart out for something you love and keep 100% of the profit.

Doing good - While this isn't exclusive to entrepreneurs, it's definitely a plus. You control where your company's profits go, and if you choose, you can allocate your financial gains to other good causes.

You can sponsor a charity, a non-profit, or just personally give back to the community. This is quite honestly one of the best parts of being an entrepreneur.

WHEN YOU START YOUR RECRUITMENT AGENCY, YOU'LL START TO REALISE THAT...

YOU DON'T NEED to work for anyone else, earning a tiny fraction of what you're truly worth...

YOU DON'T NEED to miss out on your entire life, because 5-6 days a week you're getting up in the early hours to go to work, and returning home when it's dark, and only having a few weeks holidays a year for yourself...

YOU DON'T NEED to spend hours commuting to and from work, crammed onto trains or buses, or caught up in stressful, irritating traffic jams...

YOU DON'T NEED to pander to your boss in the hope that they might notice how hard you've been working and give you that long-overdue pay rise.

YOU DON'T NEED to spend your entire week counting down the hours until THE WEEKEND!

YOU DON'T NEED to do any of that, because the opportunity for something different... something better, is right here, right now...

There's no need to work for other people when it's so straightforward to set up your own business from home and tap into the enormous money-making potential of the internet.

And in my recruitment start-up Home Study masterclass coaching and training programme, I'm going to be showing you exactly how to do it so that you transform your life, just as I have helped hundreds of my new start-ups to do.

And believe me, when I say this programme has everything you need to make that happen.

Taking the Plunge

So, what does it take? First, let's look at what it doesn't take. You don't need an MBA or high-powered business background, and you don't need to be rich or to take a second mortgage on your home.

Leaving the rat race is not as daunting as it may seem. You'll look back in later years and marvel at how easy it was and how much you gained for a relatively little cost.

Many of the greatest entrepreneurs of our time began their business with no advanced degrees and hardly any start-up capital.

But make no mistake about it: What you save in cash capital you will initially need to make up for in sweat equity and passion.

The major investment in most self-owned businesses certainly in the initial stages is an investment of oneself in the form of time, focus, and persistence.

You don't need to be a genius at negotiation or a whiz at numbers. You just need a proven and tested training programme, a mentor, and coach to guide you along the way, and purpose fuelled by a strong dose of drive and commitment!

So, ask yourself this question...

Can you really afford to miss out on the incredible opportunity that lies in front of you right now?

If you have any real ambitions to launch a home-based recruitment business and make REAL money online, this programme has everything you need to do it and more.

In other words, you have your recruitment agency set up your website ready to attract candidates, your contact management database in place and all the sales and marketing literature you need to drive business to your organisation.

Remember, this is all about baby steps taking that first action and building on that action and gradually improving and creating a lifestyle you deserve.

And now, if you are ready to have that kind of success, then your next step is to book in for one of my free recruitment start-up training programmes by visiting www.recruitmentagencyrevolution.com/join.

Now you have a decision to make. I can't make it for you.

The only thing I can assure you is that there could never be a better time to start your home-based recruitment agency because you are ahead of the curve and where you can once again quite simply be the iTunes of the recruitment industry if you act today, right now.

Rest assured that this business model absolutely works and can work for you.

The bottom line is that with my Recruitment Startup Programme, you'll never be left on your own, unsure of what to do next.

The programme explains EXACTLY what you need to do and how to do it, with practical examples, case studies, and action plans thrown in to ensure that you get your very own profitable recruitment business up and running in the shortest possible timeframe.

And don't forget, this is the same system that I've used to help all my new start-ups build their fortune with their recruitment agency. All of these methods are time-tested and proven to work.

Everything I've ever known and taught about making money in the recruitment industry – and I mean EVERYTHING – is right there in your recruitment masterclass coaching and training programme. All you need to do is watch the training videos, implement the programme, and add any questions for me to review directly with you as you go along.

And once you've got this programme in your hands, there's absolutely NO REASON why you can't precisely do what my new start-ups have been doing...

The truth is clients are desperate to save on their recruitment costs so that they can keep their business afloat.

Access to millions of candidates by using social media networks is readily available and growing every day.

And all you need to do is plug into the system, match candidates to client vacancies, and make a shed load of money in the process.

Of course, you have to learn how to run the business and do the work. You have to work the programme, but once again, the programme works.

In our 'Done For You' business model, my team and I will always be there to show how to target red-hot, hugely profitable industries that are desperately looking for top candidates...

I'll always be there to show you how to automate the various elements of the recruitment process online so that it pulls in quality candidates to place into jobs on AUTOPILOT!

I'll always be there to show you how to write powerful and persuasive sales and marketing emails that will make your clients eager to see your high-salary candidates allowing them to earn some high fee placements!

I'll always be there to show you how to utilise social media to drive hordes of candidates towards YOUR job vacancies, day after day, week after week...

I could go on, but I'm sure you catch my drift!

Hopefully, by now, you would have been convinced that there are absolutely no reasons for you not to change your life today.

In conclusion, imagine six months from now finding real financial freedom.

Imagine not having to worry about the economy or the political climate because it is unnecessary!

Imagine driving a nice car that is safe and dependable, with no monthly payments. They're paid for! Imagine that you no longer get monthly bills or calls from creditors. You owe no one money!

Imagine not having to worry about losing your home and disrupting your family or having to change their schools in the event of losing your job because you have no debt!

In life, it is very rare that ordinary people get a chance to fulfil their dreams,

but who wants to be ordinary?

So, register to attend my free online recruitment start up event right now at:

www.recruitmentagencyrevolution.com/join

Or you can contact my team on 0800 688 6277 to book to attend one of my live workshop presentations.

Once again, you don't need to have any inherent gift or specific skills; however, you must act right now!

The only ingredients that you need to add to be successful are your time and commitment.

If you give your recruitment business sufficient time and commitment, you will achieve three things that rarely go together.... you will have fun; you will benefit others, and you will make a substantial income!

The opportunity to join our 'Done For You' recruitment start-up programme is time-sensitive; therefore, you will need to act fast, right now, if you want a guarantee to get on board.

Or you will quite easily miss out, and once the places have gone, they have gone.

Ok, just contact me today and book to attend my 45-minute Recruitment Startup event; you have nothing to lose and everything to gain.

Once again, thanks for reading my book, and I look forward to hearing from you.

Visit: **RecruitmentAgencyRevolution.com/join**

You can get in touch with me by any one of these methods:

Email: info@recruitmentstartup.net

Web: www.RecruitmentAgencyRevolution.com/join

Telephone: 0800 622 6877

Skype: joe.b.davis70

CHAPTER 14

Extracts of Video Testimonials from Some of Our Amazing Clients

Here's what over 120 of our amazing clients had to say about our unique Recruitment Start-up's coaching and training programme.

"I came to Joe Davis, and the guidance he provided was immense holding my hand step by step. ***Last year we turned over £100,000 working part-time. And this year, even If we don't make a single placement from today, we are still lined up for £597,000."***

Suleman M.

"Joe took us through the process of calling clients and was key for us in being able to become confident in what we were doing. ***We made our first placement, and literally, the doors opened; we made five placements one after the other, and that was a total of £39,000 that we billed within the space of six weeks!"***

Chris P.

*"**Joe showed me how to make a placement very quickly and efficiently within 30 days**. So, for me, I could already plan how I was to obtain the money and how it would financially benefit me because there's a clear goal and strategy to follow."*

Abigail S.

*"I can honestly say; it has been the best decision I've made. Your company was true to its promise in providing me with immediate vacancies to work on, **which enabled us to make our first two placements within a fortnight of starting. BRILLIANT!"***

Faysal A.

*"After starting to work with Joe, **I made my first placement within six weeks,** which has helped me financially to move my recruitment project forward. I would definitely recommend Recruitment Startup's Services to anyone looking to get their recruitment company."*

Stephen H.

*"**My recruitment agency has been up and running for four weeks now, and we have already got back our full initial investment**. When I first looked at this business*

opportunity, I thought it looked to be good to be true, but I was completely wrong."

Joan E.

*"I'm in charge of the Care sector, anything from Carers to registered managers. It **took me roughly about four weeks to get my first placement,** from meeting clients to building up relationships with them and acquiring the candidate."*

Tariq M.

*"I manage the driving, warehouse, freight and aviation side of the business. **We have already secured contracts to supply warehouse and aviation workers both temps and perms.**"*

Mandeep U.

*"The coaching and support are second to none, and I cannot speak highly enough about the Training and support that I have received. **When I think back on all the work, I was expected to do to earn just a fraction of want I am earning; I only wished I had known about this programme a lot sooner.**"*

Brenda F.

"Obviously, Joe Davis has got a lot of experience in the industry, and he's been able to provide a lot of practical insights into how to approach clients. ***We did win contracts from them without having a hard sell over the usual recruitment agency."***

Nathaniel A.

"My goals are to go global with the help of Recruitment Start-up. Joe has done a wonderful job for us; the training is excellent. He has a lot of materials which is really fantastic, and ***I am looking at achieving my goal of hit £100,000 in the next couple of months."***

Tunde O.

"They took us right through a ***step by step process on generating leads, finding candidates, how it all works, writing contracts, everything****. Even now, five years on, we're still talking to Joe and bouncing ideas off, less than before but still there."*

Neo P.

"For a while, I had been considering whether this business opportunity could provide me with ***the right training and guidance for starting my recruitment***

business, and in all honesty, the information, tools, and training provided had a quality second to none."

George N.

"It has always been my ***ambition to set up a recruitment agency to supply staff to the UAE, Gulf and Middle Eastern market,*** *especially as the potential for business is huge. To say I am impressed with the* ***speed in which Recruitment Start-up has established our business is an understatement."***

Abdul S.

"I would recommend those who really want to start a business in terms of Recruitment to come to this kind of a workshop. ***Once you attend it and you're willing to do it, there is a team around you to help you to start. Especially to get the vacancies."***

Terrence M.

"Yes, we were able to do that (Find a job and source a candidate). I never thought it would be that that easy. Within the space of 20 minutes, I got it. *So, I guess what I can say is if you invest time in it, then the possibilities are limitless really."*

Binna O.

"I have to ***say Joe Davis definitely has a joy and warmth and sincerity about him and really wants to make your achievements happen****. I know we'll definitely be using his tools and his expertise to help make my recruitment business happen."*

Jessica J.

"It's amazing; it has been actually very educational, especially when ***Joe goes through all the strategies on how to find clients and on how to find the candidates."***

Nathan N.

"Recruitment Start-up has offered superb support and guidance throughout. Particularly, Joe Davis, *there are times when you have doubts if you can do this or not, but a visit to him will clear all your doubts, and you will be on your way."*

Amit M.

"Me starting this now has opened my eyes and ***showed me where I could gain a lot of money, more time for my family also to help other people who are seeking employment.*** *So that's what I stand for, and I am very grateful."*

Charmaine J.

*"**Joe is exceptionally good with what he does.** He goes straight to the point; **he tells you what it is, how to get this done** and where to find relevant information in a clear, concise way."*

Solomon T.

*"He just made one phone call, and when I heard him talking about it the last time I didn't believe him, It was too good to be true, but **today I witnessed that myself because he did make that one phone call, and it went through, and it was just mind-blowing.**"*

Allan M.

*"This workshop gives me ambition, **also enough information for me to see 360 degrees how it works.** It was amazing, really; everyone should come and see it."*

Mohammed H.

"I'm a lawyer by profession and businessman. Well, its

*information is quite informative, quite in-depth. **He knows what he's talking about, you know, he knows the stuff.**"*

Jerry S.

"I've always wanted to set up my own, my own business. Part of the workshop is mostly the presentation of Mr Davis. ***Yes, in fact when I get home, I will tell my family all about it. It was enjoyable and well produced."***

Ben O.

"I started my recruitment business for catering and hospitality and to get all the support. ***I have had all problems clarified for sure for my business to go on and achieve my goal."***

Maria Rosa S.

"Joe and his team are very knowledgeable, and they offered us a lot of help. They've been supportive in terms of what it is we need to be doing on a daily ***basis. I would definitely recommend them if you want to have a successful business."***

Rhoda F.

"I would definitely recommend Recruitment Start-up if you're thinking of starting up a recruitment agency. ***I think it saves you time and money ultimately because***

you can actually develop your agency much quicker *and have the expertise on top."*

Jan F.

"I like the Testaments from people about what they have acquired within a certain short space of time. ***It sounds good, and it sounds like fast money, but it's legal, and that was quite interesting."***

Anthea S.

"It's good to have someone who has the depth of knowledge of what the business is about. And this is Joe. *Someone who's been in the business for over 30 years and he has the in-depth knowledge of what it takes you to get there."*

Remi S.

"This workshop is excellent and very useful for online business. *I have enjoyed the very good talk from Joe. He gave us very nice information on how we can earn money."*

Anand R.

"I started to give these guys here, particularly Joe, ago and it's been fantastic. The staff are very friendly, and the actual value that they've added to my peace of mind. ***I've attended plenty of events, and none of them has come remotely close to adding this amount of value."***

Charlton N.

"Having the opportunity of getting ***the expertise of someone with 40 years of experience in the field, I would consider it a great asset*** *and a great motivation to taking the first step into starting your own business."*

Marilena B.

"One of the reasons that have been stopping me from starting my own agency is actually fear of lack of information. ***But today is like; I don't know my eyes is opened, just really, really opened.*** *I am so glad that I actually met Joe today."*

Jane N.

"Joe, as everybody knows, has a long-established background in Recruitment. So, like any other ***business, if you've got somebody there who can show you all the pitfalls, hold your hand, walk you through the door, that's so helpful to me."***

Ajit J.

"Joe has helped us all the way from day one setting up a business and recruiting staff. ***And knowing that 35 years' experience is on the other side of the phone is something that you need when you first start-up,*** *and that's what exactly Joe did."*

Sandeep K.

"We were confident in ourselves but not confident in the information that we had. ***Just basically being able to access to information that you can't get on the internet or any sort of book*** *that we've tried to look for in terms of setting up a recruitment agency."*

Olivia H.

"I work for a private company, and I work very long shifts, and my company recently made a profit of 81 billion pounds. So, I think with all the hard work that I put in, ***even if I put half as much into my own agency, I feel I can get a slice of whatever profits everyone else is making."***

Kudzai S.

"I actually was considering starting a business myself, and I think this ***answered all my questions, particularly***

considering my age because you are never too old to start. *I've enjoyed the workshop very much. It has motivated me to want to start a recruitment agency."*

Carol W.

"I came here because after some time on the job- ***seeking, I was feeling kind of discriminated in the job market.*** *I'm quite positive I have some very precious insights on this DVD which I just got from the workshop.* ***Not to mention Joe was absolutely brilliant."***

Diana P.

"We needed to get the logistics of it before we could go on and continue doing what we wanted. ***I feel quite confident that Joe is actually the one to give us the support; we are quite excited about starting."***

Louise H.

"On listening to the workshop, I decided that this is the right thing for me. ***I came in for one to one training, with him showing me how to make calls, in getting contracts and getting clients****. And then I did get one client."*

Doreen C.

"The explanations of the job they received was excellent, and I start doing my job. ***You're having backstage someone to help you through your set up.*** *And you can do what you want to do."*

Gabriel D.

*"**They start absolutely everything, how to find the clients, how to present your clients,** how to contact the businesses with so many options."*

Maria H.

"It was just, pretty much to the point where you can take that next step in making the business happen. ***Yes, it's very informative, it's very helpful, and I found walking away feeling very confident and happy."***

Christine A.

"I was privileged to have attended the start-up of your own recruitment agency. It was very informative. ***You get to gain financial freedom. You are able to start and work at your own pace; you have that freedom."***

Sylvia C.

"I'm definitely more confident about setting up a recruitment agency after this workshop. It has answered quite a few questions. ***This will be my first port of call, and I would definitely recommend putting a deposit down and having Joe guide you.*** *Otherwise, you could try it on your own without any guidance and failed."*

Victor G.

"If Recruitment is what you want to go into, this is the place to do it. *I found it clear, easy to understand. I went over it again so that you can take in what is given you."*

Theresa M.

"I found this is exactly what I need to take the next step forward. ***There's so much inside information that I didn't really know what was possible until now."***

Michael J.

"Joe showed us the kind of industry you can actually go into to recruit. Financial forecasting, testimonies of other people. ***He actually showed how getting that's been successful.*** *I think anyone interested in Recruitment should come to see Joe's presentation and speak to him as well."*

Mujib R.

"I just attended the seminar, and what I like best about it was, ***he actually really gave ideas on how to do a whole phone call with your potential candidate and your potential clients."***

Diana P.

"The thing I enjoyed about the workshop ***was I was able to get a lot of information, just the way to go about getting your clients and the way to just building your recruitment empire."***

Jessica J.

"I would highly recommend people to come to this workshop, understand how the business goes. ***I had like 50 per cent information before, but the confusion I had in my mind's been mostly cleared today."***

Mohammed H.

"I have been armed with facts and knowledge on how I can do a lot of things that ***I didn't really even think existed in the most simplest way."***

George O.

"I was able to get a lot of information just ***what you need to know to go about getting your clients and the way to just build your recruitment Empire."***

Kenneth M.

"My personal goals for the future is that I want to be working for myself. ***I want to pick and choose when I want to work, and working for an employer; you can't do that."***

Sylvia G.

"We plan to, first of all, use this model in the UK and later on, we're planning ***to transfer the model to other different countries as for example, like East Africa and the United States."***

Samuel A.

"Today, we have one of twelve one-to-one sessions with a mentor to help us through the process of the business, ***which is really an important step when you are going out and starting a business on your own with limited knowledge."***

Chloe V.

"Joe has been great for us because at the beginning we were literally on the phone probably every day, and ***Joe***

would have a combination of things that help us with would give us information *he'd give us training he would point us in the right direction."*

Rachel P.

"I've benefited financially the sense that it was financial income, additional income for me. ***I mean, it has opened my eyes to see that there is a viable alternative to getting the money, where you can become financially independent."***

Chris A.

"It's definitely for somebody who is a go-getter that wants to go out there and doesn't want to do a nine-to-five and is

fed up of working for somebody else. ***I don't like being told what to do, and I have an entrepreneurial mindset in order to get what I want."***

Yasmin T.

"I am studying for a Masters in London; I am a young entrepreneur, ***and I will be starting my own business, and having met with Joe, I would definitely recommend his services."***

Malik A.

"I was blown over by the Training straight away. *I realized it's something that I want to do. I want to start my own business and what but what better recruitment business especially in the fields that I'm interested in."*

Karen S.

"I will recommend Recruitment Start-up to everybody that

I know who wants to start a business ***because I think it's a very good business, and you can make a lot of money."***

Francis E.

"It's amazing; it has been actually very educational, especially when ***Joe goes through all the strategies on how to find clients and on how to find the candidates."***

Angeline M.

"He gave us solid experience that he has all with all these years and delivered the *whole presentation in a way that we all understood. Recommended completely! 100%."*

Patricia G.

"I attended the workshop because I have been thinking about starting my recruitment agency for years. ***The***

information made me more confident that I can do it, I can

start my agency."

Albena K.

"It quite amazed me that Mr Davis has held my attention which is rare and for that length of time and basically has simplified what is an intricate business. ***I think everyone should have this experience once in a lifetime."***

Pamela R.

"I have a personal interest in the recruitment business; I like that you can run it on a low-cost budget from your house or on the move. ***That's why it's quite logical and easy to run the business. It was very thorough and extremely well Presented."***

Kumar T.

"I like the testaments from people about what they have acquired within a short space of time. ***It sounds good, and it sounds like fast money, but it's legal, and that was quite interesting."***

A Smith.

"The presenter was very good, knowledgeable, seems to know the stuff. ***The fact that he had 30 years' experience in Recruitment was evident. So yeah, really good."***

Nana A.

"The presentation was very good. ***I like the use of feedback from people who've been on the program as well.*** *So, there's insight on what the benefits they got from it, from the presentation and the training."*

Christopher A.

"I really enjoyed the seminar today because I feel that Joe Davis took his time to teach us the things he has learned in his experience as being a recruitment agent*. I feel confident enough to at least give it a go."*

Abigail O.

*"This is something I've been thinking about for a very long time****, so I'm actually really excited to think that I am going to start*** *and that there's that possibility to get perfect help to start."*

Agnes W.

*"I decided to come for the training and see what the training is all about****. And by coming to this event, I've***

heard so much that it has now motivated me to start tomorrow."

Fola D.

"My fear was how to start the business. ***However, the information I have received made me see that this is where you can come too and get everything you need*** *if you want to move your business up."*

Kingsley A.

"People need to come to one of Joe's introduction event and just to hear and see that he has gone over and beyond the call of duty *by the resource materials, the support that he gives, answering questions as well that you might have."*

Christine A.

"I am going to sing this out loud for people who don't know what line of business to go in; this is where you need to be. *This is guaranteed success literally because they're holding your hands all the way you're not left on your own. I would recommend it to anybody."*

George L.

"I work as a nurse. And I always felt like if I had my own business, I'd be able to have my own time and obviously

have extra money. ***But today, it just dawned on me that it is it can become a reality.*** *And I felt very, very encouraged to understand how from Joe."*

Monica P.

*"**Joe is a very knowledgeable person in the field, and that has really increased my confidence.** And by the end of the session, all my questions have been answered, such that I didn't have a question to ask at this moment in time."*

Rosemary K.

"I came over as a novice, but right now, I feel that I now have what it takes, with the help of Joe Davis, to move ahead *and have my own recruitment agency. I would recommend this for anybody who is looking to get started."*

Sam C.

"I've always had an interest in Recruitment, especially in the field of technology, so I attended recruitment workshop to gain a better understanding of the industry, ***and I found the information provided by Joe was***

fantastic and definitely had provided me everything I needed to know to get started."

Tunde H.

"The one to one was the best part for me because ***Joe showed me with just one phone call how easy it can be to get a client and a candidate to suit the vacancy.*** *The service was fantastic, and if you devote time to it and do it well, it is a lucrative business."*

Gladys O.

"I attended joes' workshop, it's amazing, a lot of positive energy. It's given me lots of information about the recruitment industry and the process. ***I will recommend it to anyone who is looking to start their own agency."***

Dhaneesh F.

"I attended Recruitment Startup's Workshop, and I love every bit of the training. Quite happy to start after listening to the whole programme and the benefits attached to it. ***Very genuine! Highly recommended. That's why I give it a 5 Star."***

Evelyn D.

"My experience with Recruitment Start-up is mind-blowing from the workshop up to the actual one to one training. ***I am now able to start the recruitment business despite all the doubts.*** *I am so grateful."*

Godspower O.

"I loved every bit of the training; it was literally fantastic; that was a big jump for me. ***I was again amazed to see that with one training session, how to obtain and place candidates, never thought I could handle this, but now it's just like all at my fingertips."***

Tahir M.

"I am pleased with my first training session as Joe was able to make a placement from our first phone call. *I was sceptical in the beginning, but Joe proved me wrong. It was a great experience. I will highly recommend this great opportunity."*

George H.

"Joe ***demonstrated through a telephone call not only how to get a vacancy but also candidate;*** *that demonstration was capital in building my confidence."*

Troh F.

"This is more than I expected. The workshop was brilliant, well put together and definitely answered most, if not all, the questions. I will not hesitate to recommend Joe Davis highly. ***He knows the industry no end! If only we could give six stars!"***

Sherri B.

"Joe presented excellently with essential information punctuated with real-life experience. ***I definitely feel fired up and ready to go with my plan to start a recruitment agency."***

Charmayne M.

"Today, I attended the Recruitment Start-up workshop given by Joe Davis, ***which was so informative and an excellent insight to how the recruitment industry works.*** *He made me feel comfortable and welcoming; also, he encouraged us all to engage with each other. Can't wait to start."*

Nae J.

"I have been for some time now thinking of starting something that would give me the chance to help others, but also allow me to be financially free from the

9-5 life. ***This workshop alone has provided me with a framework, which has been tested to work."***

Chinelo A.

"This is the opportunity that I have waited five years for; ***I am so grateful to be part of this insightful recruitment training by Joe Davis.*** *It was an eye-opener; Joe is an experienced practitioner with a wealth of knowledge and skills in Recruitment."*

John O.

"Mind-blowing presentation. ***This really opened up my mind to the world of being a recruitment business owner!*** *Joe is a remarkable individual that communicated excellently. Detailed and informed with an honest approach. Highly Recommended!"*

Max J.

"My long term goal is to employ people internationally, to work in Dubai, Africa and Ghana, where the oil business is there and growing. ***I would recommend people to use the services of Recruitment Start-up; they are there to help you to achieve your goal."***

Lilly W.

"Joe has given us the necessary training. Demonstrating ***ways of making money, and to be financially independent,*** *as well as the testimonials of people who have testified of their satisfaction in their earning powers."*

Rosemary T.

*"**The feeling of running your own company is quite uplifting and fulfilling** as I am personally tired of working for other people and making them rich. Joe is really very good at what he's doing, and I'm very grateful to him."*

Michael O.

*"The recruitment start-up workshop has been great. **I was amazed how quickly one can start earning after starting and the kind of support available** to help me hit the ground running."*

Dauda O.

*"I had a passion for starting my own recruitment agency but had no clue how to start. **The training was an eye-opener and a beginning of a greater height for me.** I*

was so enthused that I could not wait to start my own recruiting agency."

Lola O.

"Most appropriate value judgement and senses of priorities. ***They put customers interests and concerns first. Exemplary training services."***

Seton D.

"Joe is a very experienced man who can explain in more details how to start your own recruitment agency. ***He is more open and can really tell you in detail on how to do it and is very open to all and answers all the questions being raised."***

Vusi U.

"I found the workshop very informative and helped to build confidence up. *Mr Joe Davis approach is very friendly, and I was impressed with his explanation with empirical evidences."*

Yadav S.

"We are appreciative of the ***continuous support that we get from Recruitment Start-up with personal and one***

***to one mentoring we got from the Director** - Joe Davis and his dynamic team."*

Adeleke A.

***"The workshop was very educational! It was to the point; this is an opportunity I would advise others not to miss out on.** Joe left no stone unturned as he took us through both the good and downsides of starting up one's own recruitment company."*

Zaza T.

*"I was motivated to start my own business, as I have been working in health care for so many years. I have just finished my MBA in healthcare, and **I was looking for work, but decided instead to open my own recruitment agency.**"*

Angela C.

*"The training has been very informative; I have learned so much about the recruitment industry. I have started, and by the grace of God, **I'm encouraging anyone out there who is at a crossroad to attend the recruitment start-up presentation.**"*

Tessy O.

"You need to have the right support behind you when you are running and setting up a business. This, to me, is the key that makes your business most trusted and stable. ***And someone who is just a phone call away makes all the difference."***

Yeukai T.

"I got my training directly from Joe Davis; he showed me how to contact the client and get the vacancies. ***I was surprised that on his very first call, he was able to pick up vacancies.*** *It's quite amazing and has given me the confidence through his friendly training."*

Mobassher F.

"The training I receive was quite easy and well explained, *on how you can benefit from having your own recruitment company."*

Evelyn I.

"The training has been very informative, and he has given us all the support we need. ***He made calls to high profile clients and was able to pick up a job and a request for a CV straight away.*** *And he showed us how easy it is for us to do it too."*

Ehiag I.

"The business has now taken off, and we have signed contracts with most of the major accountancy firms*. You have a gift of coaching and motivating people and always being able to resolve issues in a friendly and pleasant manner."*

Chris P.

"The training is very informative, it gives all steps we need for the business, ***plus in his training, he covers things you need to avoid making sure that your business does not fail."***

W Innocent.

"This has been the most informative training session I have had. *Joe did a very good job of introducing what we need to know, how much the earning potential was, and why we need to get into this business now."*

Oluwatobi T.

"I am very pleased to have had my staff trained by your organization. Joe Davis is everything you look for in a recruitment coach. ***He made sure he listened to what I***

was looking for, identified my needs and matched them very well with the business."

Allan M.

"Joe, with his 40 years of experience in the recruitment business, ***is extremely professional, friendly, polite and genuinely wants the best for his trainees.*** *I would highly recommend Joe and his recruitment start-up team."*

Martha M.

"This was a dream I had about eight years ago, but we got stuck because we did not know the way forward. However, ***when we came for the training, that was the day we were born!*** *As they opened the door for us to embrace it."*

Naina L.

"I came to the Recruitment Startup's training conducted by Joe Davis, and it was very good. ***Information was comprehensive, directive, precise and gave one incentive to establish your own company."***

Gladys O.

"Firstly, I would like to say that the training and service you have provided us is fantastic. *You highlighted the high points and the lows of starting up in recruiting. The market I am recruiting in is a tough one, but every time we meet you, you fill us with confidence."*

Isabelle M.

ABOUT THE AUTHOR

The author, Joel Davis, has had over 40 years of experience working in the recruitment industry.

During his time in recruitment, he has worked at Director and Senior Management level for companies such as Reed Employment, Blue Arrow, Crown Personnel, and DP Connect, to name a few.

His goal is to give ordinary people, from all backgrounds and walks of life the opportunity to have their share of the recruitments £35 billion industry, so that it is for the many not just the few.

To find out more, please visit

www.recruitmentagencyrevolution.com/join

where you can watch a free online event, plus book a call directly with Joel to discuss this unique opportunity in greater detail.

Joe Davis FIRP

Author

Once again, thanks for reading my book, and I look forward to hearing from you.

Visit RecruitmentAgencyRevolution.com/join

You can get in touch with me by any one of these methods:

Email: info@recruitmentstartup.net

Web: www.RecruitmentAgencyRevolution.com/join

Telephone: 0800 622 6877

Skype: joe.b.davis70